A GRAYWOLF DISCOVERY

Graywolf Discovery books are books we love,
the sort of treasure an enthusiastic reader passes along to friends.
We've discovered some of these ourselves, but most
have been recommended to us by authors, booksellers, or other
members of the family of book-nuts.

The Men
in
My Life

And Other More or Less True Recollections of Kinship

JAMES D. HOUSTON

Graywolf Press

Some of these pieces have appeared previously in *Zyzzyva*, *The Threepenny Review*, *West* Magazine, *The Paper* (Honolulu), the *Yes!* Capra Chapbook, *Three Songs for my Father*, and in the collections, *West of the West*, *Roots and Branches*, *Stories and Poems from Close to Home*, and *California Childhood*.

Publication of this volume is made possible in part by a grant provided by the Minnesota State Arts Board through an appropriation by the Minnesota State Legislature, and by a grant from the National Endowment for the Arts. Significant additional support has been provided by the Andrew W. Mellon Foundation, the Lila Wallace-Reader's Digest Fund, the McKnight Foundation, and other generous contributions from foundations, corporations, and individuals. Graywolf Press is a member agency of United Arts, Saint Paul. To these organizations and individuals who make our work possible, we offer heartfelt thanks.

Published by GRAYWOLF PRESS
2402 University Avenue, Suite 203
Saint Paul, Minnesota 55114
All rights reserved. Printed in the United States of America.

9 8 7 6 5 4 3 2
First Graywolf Printing, 1994

Library of Congress Cataloging-in-Publication Date
Houston, James D.
    The men in my life, and other more or less true
    recollections of kinship : essays / by James D. Houston
      p. cm.- (A Graywolf Discovery)
    Includes bibliographical references.
    ISBN 1-55597-206-3 (paper)
      1. Houston, James D. -Biography. 2. Authors, American-20th century-
    Biography. I. Title. II. Series.
PS3558.087Z469 1994
813' .54-dc20   93-32683

Cover and series design by Foos Rowntree
Cover art: *Old Man, Spruce Head near Port Clyde, Maine*, *c.*1960 detail of photo by Berenice Abbott/Commerce Graphics Ltd, Inc.

CONTENTS

Remembering my father, Albert Dudley Houston, who started life in Durant, Oklahoma, in 1904, and came to rest in Santa Clara Valley in 1969.

The way that leads forward seems to
lead backward.

-Lao Tzu

You git a line and I'll git a pole, honey.
You git a line and I'll git a pole, babe.
You git a line and I'll git a pole,
and we'll go down to the crawdad hole,
honey, baby mine.

-Traditional

The Men in My Life

The Hip Plumber: A Prologue

The hip plumber is underneath my sink, squeezed in between the flung-wide cabinet doors, working with his wrench to unscrew the trap so he can unplug the drain.

"Sometimes," he says, "when I am up under here all by myself, in the shadows with the pipes and the smells, I think what the hell am I doing in a situation like this? And then I just relax and say to myself, It's okay. It's okay to be here. This is where I am supposed to be. If I wasn't supposed to be here, I wouldn't be here. You know what I mean? What I am saying is, I surrender to that place and that time, and then I am at peace with it, I become one with it. Hand me that flashlight now, so I can see what the hell is in here."

I hand him the flash and he peers around at the stuccoed underbelly of the sink, the chalky corrosion stains.

"I don't take any of this seriously," he says. "I mean, it has to be fun. I have to enjoy it. I go out on one of these big jobs, where some contractor calls me in to do the whole kitchen and bathroom, and these other guys are out there, the roofers, the sheetrock guys. They're glum. They're walking around doing what they do, but they can't wait for the day to end. And me? I'm singing, I'm smiling. They say, Hey, you don't have any right to smile, doing this kind of shitwork. In their view, see, anybody who smiles must not know what he's got himself into. They think something is wrong with me because I really do enjoy *what I'm doing. But hey, it's all one, isn't it? Work is worship. That's what I tell them out there on the big construction jobs. I say, Work is worship. They just look at me."*

Now he has the pipes loose, and he is feeding the snake-cable down into the long drain, a few inches at a time, feeding, cranking the spool-handle ferociously, then feeding a few more inches of cable.

"You see, I am just a puppet. This came to me nine years ago. I saw that what I had to do was surrender myself to . . . whatever you want to call it. God. Brahman. The Great Force. The Over-soul. You name it. I call it God. But you know what I mean. You surrender to it. You are a puppet, and it works through you. Each morning I wake up, and I think to myself, Okay, what is important. Feel good. That is the first thing. Then, Share it. Share what you feel. And surrender to whatever comes your way. Look at this snake. You know what it's doing? It's flopping around down there at the bottom of your pipe where all the gunk has accumulated. There is nothing wrong with your drain pipe, by the way—although I might re-plumb this trap for you one of these days, if you're into that. You have about a ten-inch loop here, and all you need is four, otherwise you have water standing on both sides of ten inches, plus these two extra fittings you really don't need. Who installed this stuff anyhow?"

I tell him it came with the house. He inspects the loop, eyes wide in the half-dark. He shifts his position. He gives the handle another crank, with another smile, the fun-lover's grin, playful, a prankster.

"What I'm saying is, the drain pipe is innocent. The drain just does what it has to do, which is be a pipe for the water. And the water does what it has to do, which is swirl as it descends, so that over the years it coats the inside of the pipe with all the little pieces of stuff that come down out of the sink, and this makes a kind of doughnut inside the pipe, a doughnut with a hole through the middle that gets a little bit smaller year by year. The doughnut gets bigger, and the hole gets smaller and smaller and smaller, until it is down to a very fine point—which is just like meditation, you see. But then one day, bip,

the little hole closes. The drain stops draining, and the snake goes down there and opens it up, like the kundalini snake of break-through perception! And whammo, a channel is cleared and the water is flowing again!"

Part One:
LESSONS, EARLY AND LATE

Prunepicker

It was the first day of pre-season practice and I was standing next to Buster, suiting up. We had lockers side by side but this happened to be the first time we had seen each other unclothed. He was watching me lace my hip pads. With what I took to be an appreciative little grin he said, "You're a husky sumbitch."

My laugh came out high, betraying me. I was seventeen, a very green and nervous and insecure freshman. He was twenty-four. He had served in World War Two and he was still in college, playing out his final year of eligibility. His name was not Buster, but that's what I'm going to call him, because it fits what he did to me, or for me. Next to Buster Budlong I did not feel very husky at all. I weighed around 170 in those days, a lean and lanky six foot two. He was taller by a couple of inches, and much thicker. He had thick bones covered with leathery muscular skin, and on his head a cap of brown hair made of bristles that in my memory were so short and stiff he could easily have played without a helmet.

"You must of been a tackle in highschool," he said.

"Fullback," I said. "Blocking back most of the time."

"Out there in prunepicker country?"

His eyes challenged mine. His mouth curved in a self-satisfied grin. I tried to match it with a grin of my own. I had been in west Texas about a week, and I was already weary of these cornball jokes about California. But I wasn't saying anything yet, still uncertain where to draw the line between kidding around and insult.

When all the laces were tight, I followed him to the door. The sky was rosey with a dawn cloud cover. The air was heavy. It was so hot, in mid-August, we had to get up at 4:30 and practice from 5:30 to 7:30, then sweat somewhere until sundown when we would practice again. We stepped out into the heat and walked together across the cinder track toward the field. It was patched here and there with pale green, but most of what had once been grass was as dry and bristled as the short hair on Buster's head.

A blocking sled stood at the edge of the field. Just for the hell of it, he dipped and ran at the sled and threw a shoulder into the raggedy pad, more metal backing now than stuffed canvas. He began shoving it across the field, making the whole weighted sled jump with each punch of his enormous shoulder.

"Hyah!" he would shout as he lunged. "Hyah! Hyah! Hyah!"

"Hey, look at ol Buster," one of the backs called out. "What'd you have for breakfast this mornin, Buster?"

"I aint had breakfast yet. Gonna have me a prunepicker for breakfast."

The back laughed, swinging his arms. Waiting for the coach to call us together, he had a few moments to play Buster's straight man. "Well now, just how do you recognize a prunepicker when you see one?"

Buster pushed away from the sled and stood up with his hands on his hips. "You look at the eyes," he said. "There's only two kinds of people from California—

prunepickers, and movie stars. And movie stars always wear dark glasses."

This line, which I had already heard four or five times, drew some chuckles from players moving past us toward mid-field where the head coach now stood, in his t-shirt and his sweatpants and his billcap. We jogged over there and ganged around to listen to the morning's agenda—warm-ups, wind-sprints, blocking sled for the linemen, pass drill for the backs and ends, with thirty minutes of light scrimmage to run through some plays we had seen last night on the chalkboard.

This was Abilene Christian College, 1951. There was no freshman squad, no junior varsity. We all worked out together, and you were either on the varsity or you were not. In this league I was too slow to do what I had done in highschool in San Jose the previous season, although I did not know this until the day I arrived, until I stepped out of the Trailways bus that had carried me across Arizona and New Mexico, to meet the coach and meet his eyes as he sized me up. Someone had sent him my best times in the fifty and the hundred-yard dash. He was already thinking tackle, maybe defensive end. "You got the height for it, Jimbo," the coach had said, steady-eyed and fatherly. "You start puttin away enough a this good Texas food, maybe we can beef you up some by the time the season starts."

From the way I began to sweat I would have to eat and drink six times a day just to stay even. Before the warm-up calisthenics were done I was telling myself I had better take it easy until my blood thinned out. In this kind of climate you could drop from heat exhaustion by sunrise. That was my rationale for holding back in the linemen's drills, which I didn't much like. Maybe I still thought of myself as a fullback, who should not have to be doing this kind of donkeywork. Maybe a little arrogance showed as I approached the sled. Maybe that had something to to with why Buster did what he did. Knowing how he thought and how he measured people, I suspect he figured this first day on the field was as good a day as any to teach me my first lesson.

When it came time for the scrimmage that ended the work-out I was crouched across from him, trying to see his eyes underneath the helmet-edge and the bushy blond brows that bunched out like awnings of solidified flesh. The first string had a new series of plays to run through. I had been put into the defensive line. As I understood it we were there mainly to remind the offense where enemy bodies would be located. This, in my experience, had been the meaning of "run-through." Buster saw it differently.

The first play was a simple hand-off that would send a running back between guard and tackle. His job was to move me out of the way, which I fully intended to allow him to do. When the ball was snapped I stepped toward him, hands out, expecting his shoulder to come at my belt in a half-speed block. But that huge shoulder rose over my hands with a ferocious thrust, followed by his elbow which cracked into the side of my chin. It lifted me and sent me sprawling backward onto the stubble.

Tears sprang to my eyes from the shock and from the rising dust. I blinked them away and looked around. No one seemed to have noticed this. It was between me and Buster, and he too seemed oblivious, standing again with his hands on his hips, gazing downfield as if to follow the ballcarrier's path. I touched my jaw, expecting blood. It felt broken, though it wasn't. Afraid to move it, I spoke through clenched teeth.

"Buster."

He looked down, as if he had forgotten I was there.

"Buster, you know you elbowed me right in the face."

The way he was squinting I still could not see his eyes.

But I could see his mouth curve into the same self-satisfied grin. "That's right, prunepicker. That's the way we play ball down here in Texas."

It had not occurred to me that the blow was deliberate. As he said this, my limbs went hollow. In that oppressive heat they were instantly filled with the cold wind of absolute fear. His eyes were ballbearings. He was made of solid rock. He outweighed me by about sixty pounds. And sometime within the next couple of minutes I was going to have to get to my feet, line up across from him again, assume the stance and take another blow like that or try to deliver one, which seemed futile, or turn tail and walk off the field, which was not really an option, though it was a fantasy I clung to for about fifteen seconds, until my saviour appeared, an angel in the form of the head coach. He evidently had witnessed this scene from the sidelines.

Buster had just taken his first step back toward the huddle when the coach threw an arm around his vast shoulder and said softly, as they walked together, "We got some money invested in this boy, Buster. We'd like him to last at least halfway through the season."

Then the coach was calling out to his backs to try that same play one more time, a little differently, pulling them toward him with a double armed wave, like a butterfly breast stroke. This gave me an extra moment to sit in the dirt and feel the numbness of my jaw begin to swell and become a throb of emerging pain and ponder how I had ended up on my butt in disgrace in the dry wind and stubble of a practice field fifteen hundred miles from home.

*

At age seventeen I had a lot of fear and confusion, but I had no answer to that question. Many years would pass before I saw how far back it went, that it was both cultural and genetic. In the America of my youth the curse of being too small was that you could not go out for football. The curse of being six foot two was that you could not avoid going out for football, for fear your very manhood would be questioned. In my case there was also the influence, perhaps I should say the deep longing, of an uncle, my favorite uncle, who in two important ways was much like Buster. He was not nearly as mean, but he too had grown up in a small west Texas town, and he too believed in football.

His friends called him Jim. His mother called him J.C. I always called him Jay. He never had a father to speak of, that is to say, my grandfather had not been a dedicated family man. When Jay was very young he had disappeared, leaving my grandmother with two kids to raise. By the time Jay started high school, in the late 1920s, she was trying to manage a quarter-section of land by herself, hiring help when she could afford it. Money was scarce in the best of times, and the land in their part of Texas had never been generous. Cotton was grandma's main crop. It took a terrible amount of work to make it pay anything at all.

Jay collected football photographs and dreamed of the day when he would be a starting player. In his spare time he lifted weights, hoping for bulk, and he would run fantasy plays in the yard in the waning dusk. He spent his freshman and sophomore seasons on the bench. The year he had a shot at making first string, as a junior, he didn't enroll. There was just too much work at home. Grandma couldn't handle it all. At age sixteen he had to drop out of high school, give up his football dreams and be the man of the family, helping her tend that quarter-section.

Later on, after they had all found their way out to the west coast and San Francisco, Jay married and had a daughter, but no sons. So when I came along I was the one

young male in our transplanted west Texas clan. All his
hopes for gridiron glory were transferred to me. Every
New Years Day he would take me to the East-West game at
Kezar Stadium. When I stayed overnight at his house he
would stuff me with syrupy, butter-soaked hotcakes and tell
me how good this was for putting power in the legs and zip
in the throwing arm.

The summer before I started highschool we took off on a
fishing trip—my dad, my uncle Jay, and a couple of the
journeyman painters dad would hire whenever he had a
big job in the city. Clear Lake was where they did most of
their fishing, two hours north of San Francisco. They
would rent a couple of motel cabins and rent a boat or two,
and we would motor out onto the lake in search of bass and
catfish. At night we would eat in a restaurant, then sit
around one of the cabins and talk and get to bed early so
we could get up early and back out onto the lake.

One of these nights after dinner Jay had had a few beers,
which made his eyes get sentimental. He sat down next to
me, talking about starting highschool in the fall, what a
great opportunity that would be and not to let it slip past
me. He was talking of course about the opportunity to play
football.

"What position you going to go out for?" he said.

We were lounging on two single beds. I was bored out of
my thirteen-year-old skull watching the four of them drink
beer. There was nothing else to do but listen or sleep, and
it was too early to sleep. This was before television. There
was a table-model radio between the beds, two chairs, a
desk with a Bible in the drawer.

"Halfback," I said, knowing that's what he wanted to
hear.

Driving up there he had talked about Glenn Davis, the
All American halfback from West Point. For three years in

the mid-1940s Davis and his running mate, Doc Blanchard—Mr. Outside and Mr. Inside—had dominated the sports pages. They were still talked about, living legends you measured other players against. "Shoot, Jimbo," Jay said, "if you go out for halfback, we'll never hear about Glenn Davis again. You'll just leave him in the shade."

He took a long sip and said to my father, who was eased back on one elbow on the other bed, "Hey Dudley, Jimbo here is gonna give em a run for their money. He just might leave ol Glenn Davis in the shade."

My father didn't care much about football one way or the other, but he went along with most of what Jay said. It was not his style to disagree outloud. When he did not react Jay escalated the prediction. "You know, Dudley, this boy here is not gonna be just any old halfback. He might turn out to be an All American. Wouldn't that be something now? If Jimbo made the All American team one a these days?"

My father nodded and smiled. "It sure would be something."

With a little shoulder punch Jay said to me, "Hey Jimbo, that really *would* be something. All American halfback. Huh? Waddya say to that!"

I looked at him. His face was turning red with more than the flush that comes from drinking. His eyes were wet, brimming. "Dammit . . ." he said, and cleared his throat, his voice filled with sudden emotion he could not control. "Dammit, Jimbo, if you made the All American team, you know what I'd do?"

Tears had started, dripping down his florid cheeks. He gripped my arm. "I'd give you a gold watch! I swear it!"

His eyes were pleading, begging me to undertake this task. At the same time his weeping eyes were proud, as if I had already done it and he had the watch in his pocket, and was ready to pull it out and surprise me with the gift that would validate the great honor I had brought to the family.

"You hear me, son? The day you make the All American team, I am gonna give you a two hundred dollar gold watch and have it engraved and it's gonna say To My Nephew Jimbo with Pride from his Uncle Jay!"

I looked down at the flimsy bedspread, unable to reply. At age thirteen I had many fantasies, but that was not among them. Even as he spoke I knew it wasn't possible. Yet his belief ran so deep, or seemed to, another part of me wanted his prediction to come true, at least be probable. For his sake. Jay had created a future that had not occurred to me before. For his sake I let it live a while.

Working out with the freshman team at Lowell Highschool in San Francisco I would sometimes see myself standing in that great line-up in the sky. Dreaming of the backfield I played guard and tackle for two seasons at Lowell. I was never very good, didn't make varsity, but I knew I would get better, I would get bigger and stronger, and with size would come miraculous new levels of ability and courage. When I was fifteen we moved from San Francisco south to Santa Clara Valley, and there my football fortunes took a lucky turn. In a school half the size, with a smaller team, I finally moved from guard to fullback, and in my senior year made first string, threw a few passable downfield blocks and scored a couple of touchdowns, the most significant being a three-yard run against San Jose High, our arch-rival, on Thanksgiving Day, before five thousand fans.

I remember lying face-down in the grass, and the blades of grass tickling my nostrils, and the rich smell of autumn grass and damp earth as I opened my eyes when the play was over. So many bodies were layered above me I could only move my head and my neck. I turned and saw the merry eyes of Roy Krickeberg right next to me. He was our powerhouse guard. He had opened the hole I had just plunged through, and we had a few seconds of comradeship and intimacy there, pressed into the grass while the bodies above us peeled away.

I said to Roy, "How far did we get?"

He said, "Your nuts are on the goal line, amigo. We just won the game."

That little moment, I realize now, was the high point of my football career. I should have quit right then. But you never know these things at the time. I had already received a letter from the athletic department at Abilene, offering me room, board and tuition. This three-yard rush, coming at the end of a season in which I had started every game, seemed to confirm the wisdom and the rightness of accepting the offer. It was, I should point out, the only such offer I received and had less to do with my ability than with the fact that my family belonged to the Church of Christ, which supported the college. I was not very brave, and I was not very fast, but in the smalltown world of Santa Clara Valley in 1950 my picture had appeared once or twice in the paper. Since a cousin of ours back in Texas knew someone who knew someone, wheels were greased and doors were opened. One morning I climbed onto a bus heading south from San Jose toward Los Angeles, where I caught another bus heading inland. Two days went by, during which the world turned drier and flatter and hotter. A week later I found myself sitting in the dust at 7 a.m. gingerly touching my injured jaw to gauge its tenderness while I watched Buster and the head coach walk back toward the offensive huddle.

Claiming to believe in Jesus, by the way, was not the

only qualification for playing on this team. Being from
Texas was equally important, or having relatives there.
Most of the players came from church families in other
nearby towns and cities. In the case of good ol boys like
Buster, whose Christian traits were sometimes hard to
identify, other virtues were carefully considered. Many
sins were forgiven if you weighed over two twenty-five or
could run the hundred in ten seconds, or both.

*

After we had trooped into the locker room to change,
then to the chow hall to shovel in the hotcakes and scram-
bled eggs and sausages, I wandered back to my dorm room
and lay down on the bed sweating and thinking. I lay there
most of the day feeling sorry for myself, feeling exiled and
excluded. I wanted to climb back on the bus that very
afternoon and leave west Texas behind. But I couldn't. It
would seem too cowardly. Something else was required,
though I didn't know quite what. Short of picking him off
with a deer rifle from a moving car, there was no way I
could imagine getting even with Buster. He was too large
and thick and thick-skinned, with the brute strength to
break my arms into tiny pieces.

I was lucky, I suppose. If he were closer to my own size
and age I would have had to challenge him immediately.
No one really expected me to. But I didn't understand that
yet. I was in turmoil, and prickly with the day's rising
heat. It made me sullen, and this became my mood for the
next week or so, bringing me a nickname. Prunepicker became Pruney, which just fed my sense of alienation, particularly when it came from Buster. Warned by the coach to
keep his elbows under control, he continued rabbit-
punching with his voice.

"Hey Pruney," he would call, as we lined up for a

charging drill, "you crouch that low so you can scoop up more prunes?"

Around the middle of the second week something happened. Call it the lighting of a slow burning fuse. Call it anger. Call it pride. One morning I hit the practice field fifteen minutes early imitating his crazy lunge at the sled, half hoping I would dislocate a shoulder. I began pushing myself in every drill, every play. On windsprints I would drive my legs until they burned, until my stomach burned with nausea, and I would vomit clear water into the dry grass. Some days we would be working out in 85 and 90 degrees. It was a badge of honor to be seen throwing up, a way to let the world know how much you cared. I began to look forward to the vomitting. I was in a kind of fever, fired by salt pills and hot dry wind. It propelled me right into our first pre-season game, officially called a scrimmage, though that was an understatement. Our opponents came from Hardin-Simmons, a crosstown rival. The main difference between this game and later games was that the coach gave everyone a chance to play.

Mine came in the second quarter. I went in on defense to replace a tackle whose shoelace had inexplicably unraveled. I was positioned just inside their left end, a fellow about my size and weight, maybe a year older, lean and wiry and looking as weathered as a Texas fence post. I was ready to overpower someone. I had reached a point of pure recklessness, and it must have shown. The moment we made eye contact I knew I had the advantage.

Their quarterback was calling signals. When the ball was snapped this rangy end came at me low, to move me farther inside, but he was not low enough. I got in under him, my legs pumping. He seemed to have no weight. With my hands and a shoulder I lifted him and threw him aside like a sack of kindling, then saw nothing but open space between me and the ball carrier, a broad, squat running back with piston legs. He had just taken a hand-off on some kind of tricky reverse that was supposed to send him skirting my end of the line. When he saw me coming, a ripple of fear crossed his chunky face. It gave me speed. By that time I was eager to hurt someone or die in the attempt. I took a bead on his belt, drove my shoulder in and we both went down in that lover's roll they call a tackle. It was the one perfect tackle of my life. If Ernest Hemingway had been reporting this game he would have described it that way: "He went in well, right under the ballcarrier's elbows, and tackled perfectly."

The back lay there for a second as if dead. Then I heard him slam the ball at the grass and mutter in self-disgust, "Shitasscocksuckerfuckheadsonofabitch."

It was a crucial play, a fourth down on our thirty with two yards to go for a first. They had tried for the yardage. Instead of gaining two they lost ten, giving us a first down with fine midfield position.

Jogging toward the sidelines I heard a chorus of shouts I thought at first were jeers. But they were shouts and hoots of praise. "Whoo-ee!" they cried, and "Atta boy, Jimbo!"

Someone slapped me on the pads. "You see ol Jimbo cut that sucker in half?"

"Lord have mercy," said someone else, "Jimbo went and turned this whole game right around."

I could only stand there and grin, my adrenalin running, until Buster appeared, loomed up next to me with a wink. He patted me on the butt and said, "Son, you done real good out there. You aint gonna be a prunepicker any more."

I was floating. I was an unknown actor suddenly surrounded with microphones, getting an Academy Award and shaking hands with John Wayne. Then Buster passed by me, moving along the sidelines. My exhilaration passed too, replaced by a deep and lonesome sadness I had no words for. I looked at his broad back and at the faces, the helmeted profiles of the others, whose eyes had turned toward the midfield action. If I had been able to say in words what I felt at that moment, it would have gone something like this: "Is that it? Is that all? To pass the test and be admitted into the lobby of this club, is that really what's required?"

I did not know what to do this feeling. I had no place to put it. I had never seen it expressed or heard it talked about. You were supposed to exult in conquest, not feel short-changed. That evening at the dinner table in the chow hall, as we celebrated our performance, I added my voice to the rounds of congratulations, even though that other voice was right behind it, the voice with no words.

*

At practice I kept pushing. On the day I made it through two hours without having to force down waves of nausea, I told myself I was finally in shape. I told myself I was ready to re-enact the same bold play in a stadium filled with cheering fans. If something like that had happened, things might have turned out differently. A few scraps of glory might have silenced the voice of the non-believer, or put it on hold for a season or two. But this was a team of seniors who had eyes on the championship and finishing out their college years together in a blaze of victory. With no j.v. squad it was unlikely I would log any game time at all, even at tackle.

By mid-season I had brooded myself to a standstill. I should say, to a sit-still. What a pointless waste, I told myself, to be in this kind of shape and spend game after game on the bench. Yet each game spent sitting left me more inert, less inclined to move.

I was in the darkest grip of fourth-string inertia, when we came up against Carswell Air Force Base, which I remember as an entire team of men like Buster, grown men in their 20s who had re-enlisted after the war. They were known to play a vicious brand of streetfighter football. Maybe it wasn't football. From the bench it looked like hand to hand combat. At halftime they were leading 20–12, and everyone who had seen action was hurting somewhere. The ghastly silence in our locker room was broken only by the coach's announcement that, since this was a non-league game, he might soon be giving some freshman a chance to play.

During the third quarter he started glancing toward the low end of the bench. This was a night game, which made it easier to avoid his gaze. I was trying to appear intent upon the midfield carnage, watching yet not watching, when into my range of vision came Buster, limping toward us. The front of his jersey was wet with blood. His nose had turned purple. His shins were cut. From his ankles to his eyes he looked more than battered, he looked stunned. That was what hit me, the shock in his eyes.

I admired Buster, in spite of what he had done to me, perhaps because of it. He was the most formidable man I had ever spoken to. He was indestructible. Yet somewhere in that murky realm where huge bodies crash together play after play after play, he had come up against someone or something that could make his flinty eyes go hollow. If they could do this to Buster's face, what could they do to mine?

He fell onto the bench, with his feet spread and his head back while a trainer tried to stop the bleeding. I watched him staring at the sky, a wounded Goliath. And this was the moment, as terror and doubt swirled together, when my heart went out of the game. Whatever I felt I owed my uncle Jay just floated right out of me and up into the same sky Buster was gazing at, the big night-time sky above west Texas.

*

After that I dreaded the work-outs. Pure drudgery. I kept going through the motions because I was still on the team and they were paying my way, and I could not see beyond that. I could have quit, and probably should have, but it did not occur to me to quit. I was stuck. I was a football prisoner, waiting for another kind of angel to come along and rescue me the way the coach had rescued me from Buster.

When he first appeared, in the newspapers, and then on posters all over town, I did not see him as an angel. He was too familiar. He was famous. His name was Horace Heidt. He hosted a national radio show, an amateur hour known for its accordion players, Swiss bellringers, harmonica wizards. He also lent his name to a troupe that moved around the country making weekly stops, a touring vaudeville show. The best of his radio acts would appear on a variety program along with local amateur performers who had been selected in advance. By a miracle of uncanny timing Horace Heidt's travelling show came to town just when I needed it most.

In Abilene I had a shadow life, a second life, totally unconnected to football. Three nights a week I was rehearsing songs with a couple of newfound musical buddies. They happened to be Bible students, but not the somber and self-righteous kind. They liked to tell obscene stories, and they liked to sing jazzy two-beat and swing tunes from the 20s and 30s, a taste I had picked up in highschool, soon after I started fooling around with stringed instruments—bass, guitar, and the ukulele, which in those days was making the first of several comebacks. Our little trio had roughed out maybe half a dozen songs, when we saw the posters bearing the name and face of the smiling impresario, and beneath the face the beguiling phrase, TALENT SEARCH.

On audition day the basement of Abilene Highschool was mobbed with sopranos and barbershop quartets and young girls who sang hymns and young men prepared to recite the Gettysburg Address. We were there for the hell of it, we told ourselves, on the chance that we might see Horace himself. With such a crowd of hopefuls we did not really expect to make the final cut.

But we did. Three acts were chosen to perform at the civic auditorium one Saturday night in November, and suddenly I was faced with what appeared to be a painful choice. It was also the night of our Homecoming Game when, by tradition, Abilene Christian met its arch-enemy, McMurry, another local college. In this contest, more than football was at stake. McMurry was Baptist. Since their reading of the New Testament differed from ours on several key points of doctrine, the pre-game excitement was always flavored with a fierce evangelical zeal. Most of this was lost on me. I had not been around long enough to take the rivalry seriously, nor did I have strong feelings about Baptists, one way or the other, nor did I see how my presence on the sidelines could possibly affect the outcome of the game. Though I pretended to be torn, I was not.

At the civic that Saturday night we were ushered backstage to mingle with the chorus girls who sang and danced high-stepping routines between the main acts, changing costumes before our very eyes. We met a rotund and untutored baritone who was blind and wore overalls and had to be led to the microphone to sing *The Lord's Prayer.* We heard a trumpet virtuoso play *Caravan* and watched a baldheaded man imitate the voices of Humphrey Bogart and

Harry S. Truman. Then we were out there, under the blinding lights. Calling ourselves "The Jazzberries"— guitar, ukulele, and washtub bass—we gave them our smoothest numbers, *Sweet Georgia Brown, Minnie The Mermaid, Please Don't Talk About Me When I'm Gone.*

At the end of the show the audience was asked to applaud again for each of the three local acts. We walked off with fifteen dollars, coming in third, after a cowgirl singer and a French Horn soloist who won the hearts of the crowd playing *The Stars and Stripes Forever.*

The following Monday I was back in the locker room suiting up, as if nothing unusual had happened over the weekend. One part of me actually believed I could get away with this, could appear on the practice field with no questions asked. Another part of me must have known what I had created for myself and thus arranged for me to step alone into the sunlight just as the coach came around the corner of the gym.

I heard his voice before I saw him, as flat and uncompromising as the voice of a traffic cop asking to see your license and your registration. He spoke my name.

I froze, waiting.

"We missed you Saturday night."

"Yes sir. I was . . ."

"I know where you were. I saw your name in the paper."

This pleased me. I thought I heard a hint of forgiveness there. I was wrong. He was standing close, but not looking at me. He was studying the dirt, as if some explanation for my behaviour might crawl out from under the broken concrete path. The coach, it should be pointed out, was an honorable man. In his world he was successful and highly regarded, a man who had played well in highschool and in college and had coached well ever since, winning more games than he had lost. He was fair and just and direct and single-minded. On that Monday he had one goal in life, which was to bring in another championship team. In this world I had committed an unpardonable sin. Failing to suit up for the Homecoming Game? I may as well have taken a flatbed truck with loudspeakers down the main street of Abilene blaspheming the name of the Lord and all twelve Apostles.

Gazing at the ground he said, "Looks to me like you might have other things in life more important to you than football."

I considered lying, or inventing an elaborate alibi. I thought of pleading for a second chance. That is what the moment called for. But my mind went blank.

I said, "I guess it does look that way, yes."

His eyes turned toward me, cold, disappointed. "Then I suppose that's all you and I have to say to each other."

It was. I never saw him again, nor do I remember seeing Buster again after that day, except in dreams.

The coach walked on toward the field. I walked back to an empty locker room and took the pads and cleats off for the final time and changed into my street clothes. I had just been ex-communicated. I should have felt guilt, or shame, or failure. But I didn't. For a few hours I felt nothing. I was numb, in shock. Distantly I worried about money, about how to break this news to my family, to uncle Jay, to the cousin who had wangled the scholarship. It took me three full days to realize, to admit what a burden had been lifted from my shoulders, a nine-hundred pound anvil I had been carrying around for half my life. It was a form of weight loss, almost an out-of-body experience. I was airborne. I was freed from something I did not even suspect had been holding me captive. I had been released.

*

For a long time I thought that was the end of this story. One Sunday afternoon about thirty years later I discovered that it has no end. I was back in northern California, where I have lived most of my life, before and after the Texas interlude, and we were watching the playoffs. My wife said, "Why are we watching this?"

I said, "Wait a minute, they're getting ready to score."

At the next time-out she went over and turned the sound down and said, "It's a very male thing, isn't it."

"What is?"

"Watching football."

"Women watch football."

"Not very many. Not the way men do. What's going on? Is it the violence?"

"This isn't violent," I said. "*The Godfather* is violent. The ten o'clock news is violent."

"Well, what's the big attraction? A bunch of grown men throwing a ball around. You see something I don't see?"

"I see what everybody sees. It's right there on the screen. I'm turning the sound up now, okay? They're going for a field goal."

This was January 1982. The San Francisco 49ers were playing the Dallas Cowboys for the conference championship. The winner would go to the superbowl. Ray Wersching, the great 49ers place-kicker, was trying for a score from thirty yards out. I remember that later in the day Joe Montana's final pass seemed too high above the end zone for anyone to catch and Dwight Clark, who is six foot four, made a superhuman effort, leaped and caught the ball landing inbounds and on his feet in the last seconds of the fourth quarter, to clinch both the game and the bowl trip. But I have no memory of Wersching and this mid-game field goal attempt. As the teams lined up, a recurring dream began to roll across my inner screen. Though I had dreamed it many times, I had never before recalled it during my waking hours.

In this dream I am back in west Texas, and I am suiting up again. The time is now. I have not played in thirty years. I am out of shape, and I am scared. I am wearing pads and cleats, and we are warming up before the Homecoming Game. I am here as a returning alumnus. They have asked me to play in this game hoping my presence on the field will draw a large crowd. I like this part of it. I too am hoping my presence will draw a crowd. This is the only reason I have agreed to suit up. I am feverish with heat and squirming against the rub of the unfamiliar pads and giddy with terror. I know that if I have to carry the ball, or mix it up in any way, I will get badly injured. I mention to the quarterback that I am not as young as I used to be. When he looks at me I see that he is the same quarterback, and he is still the same age. I look around. It is the same team. I am older. They are not. The quarterback grins cryptically. "Take it easy, prunepicker, don't worry, we have thought of that."

The plays they have worked out for me, he says, are end sweeps, which will give our blockers plenty of time to cut down the defense, or tire them out, so that by the time they get to me they won't be so energetic, they won't be hitting that hard. "It won't be too bad," he says. I know I could live with this strategy, but I do not trust the quarterback. In the old days he and I were once interested in the same girl. Maybe we still are. No matter what he says, I know he is going to send me over center, or off-tackle, and I can already feel the armored bodies of the hulking Texas linemen who recognize me and will be waiting with knees and fists.

I was not surprised that such a dream should come to the

surface during the 49ers/Dallas game. In my inner history Texas and football have always been linked. The surprise was discovering that whenever I watch a football game, college or pro, Dallas or Chicago or UCLA, part of me returns to Abilene, has been returning, time and time again. Like the dream figure, a man of my age continually returns to the field of thirty-five years ago. For a few seconds they merge, they are one, the dream and the figures on the television screen. This never lasts long. Soon after kickoff the dream players dissolve, and with them all memory of fear. Then I am a fan again, one among millions, watching a game. My wife wants to know why, and she would prefer a general answer. I don't have a general answer. I can only speak for myself. I watch with wonder now, true wonder at what men will pursue and believe in—Dwight Clark's catch: an act of faith—and I watch on behalf of my uncle Jay, who has already been gone a dozen years. I suppose the watching is one way of paying tribute to this man, my favorite and most influential uncle, who loved the game as only Texans can, who believed in football with all his heart and never had the chance to play.

How Playing Country Music Taught Me To Love My Dad

Deep within my heart
lies a melody,
a song of old San Antone . . .
    —Bob Wills—

I grew up listening to my father play the steel guitar. It was his pastime and his passion. Once or twice a month our front room would fill with fiddlers and guitar pickers who had come west from Texas and Oklahoma and Arkansas and other places farther south to make money in the fields and in the shipyards of World War Two. Dad was more or less the leader, since he had the most equipment—a little speaker, two mikes, an old Westinghouse recording machine. From upstairs, with my head and my radio under pillows and covers, where I was trying to concentrate on *The Shadow*, I could hear them ripping into *San Antonio Rose* or *Detour—There's a Muddy Road Ahead*. Clutching the radio I would groan and burrow deeper and, to fend off the guitars, imagine the look of The Shadow himself, my sinister and worldly night-time companion.

I thought I was groaning about the music. But it was dad who made me cringe. Coming of age in San

Francisco, I was a smartass city kid, cool and sullen, and ashamed of all his downhome tastes and habits. During those years I lost a tremendous amount, resisting the things he cared about and denying who he was. At the time I had no way of knowing how much was working against us. No two points of origin could have been farther apart.

His hometown was not a town at all. It was an east Texas village called Pecan Gap, where kids grew up chopping cotton. To escape he dropped out of highschool in the tenth grade and joined the Navy, on a hitch that sent him to Honolulu in the mid-1920s, for two years of submarine duty at Pearl Harbor. That was where he learned half the music he knew. In Texas he had learned enough rhythm guitar to accompany singing. Some Hawaiian taught him the flat-lap style, the right hand flashing with silver picks, the left moving its little steel bar across the strings, sliding, whining, yearning, dreaming. Until the day he died, the two tunes he played most, and loved most, were *The Steel Guitar Rag* and *The Hilo March*.

He also learned the ukulele over there. When I was fourteen I found one hanging in his closet. My first hour of aimless plinking jangled his nerves. I knew this, and I kept it up until he grabbed the uke and told me to sit still while he taught me three chords and a basic strum, which he described as "tryin to shake somethin off the end of your fanger."

I started practicing that strum and those chords about two hours a day. After a week he hid the ukulele. One afternoon I came home from school and it was gone. First I accused my sister. Then I confronted my mother. When I told dad that his ukulele had disappeared he pursed his lips judiciously and said, "Gone, you say. Imagine that."

Who knows why he hid it? Maybe the sound I had been making, akin to the squawk of a rusty clothesline wheel, was too big a price to pay to have another musician in the family. Maybe he was getting even with me for refusing to listen to his band. I'm still not sure. We were both inexperienced at this game. He was my first and only father. I was his first and only son.

For two days I searched, and finally found the uke between the ceiling and the roof beams, shoved back under some insulation. When I came strumming into the front room, he turned red. His jaws bunched in the classic, teeth-grinding, Dust Bowler's way of holding it all inside. Then he tried to grin. With eyes lowered, he jerked his face sideways in that other classic gesture that can signify all moods from outrage to wonder. He said, "Looks like you scared it up."

Maybe this had been a little test, to measure my commitment. Before long he showed me the rest of his chords, another strum, a simple way to pick the melody to *Lovely Hula Hands*. About the time I had practiced all this to death, I graduated to the four-string banjo. I was in a neighborhood music store eyeing the long neck and stretched head and gleaming strings of a brand-new instrument, when the owner's seductive voice, from somewhere behind me, said I was welcome to do more than look. From there it was a short step to Dixieland Jazz which, in those days, around 1950, was the hottest sound in northern California. My songs were *The Muskrat Ramble* and *The Rampart Street Parade*. My new-found heroes were Louis Armstrong, Jack Teagarden, Turk Murphy, Red Nichols and His Five Pennies.

Sometimes, say late on a Saturday afternoon, I would be practicing, and I would hear dad in the front room tuning up, as if by chance. Begrudgingly I would find myself in there with him, running through the changes for one of his big production numbers, *The Steel Guitar Rag*, the *Cow Cow*

Boogie. But I was arrogant about these little rehearsals. His arrangements, his slides and flourishes, his idea of an impressive finale—this was ancient history. It was beneath me. It was worse than hicksville. It was Okie music. And I was anything but an Okie.

From Dixieland I soon moved toward modern jazz, and now my instrument was the upright bass. *How High The Moon. Darn That Dream. Willow, Weep For Me.* These were the songs you had to know, and how could dad and I even talk about such music? The tunes we listened to placed us on opposite sides of an uncrossable chasm, a Grand Canyon of taste—the augmented seventh chord as far from his vocabulary as a queen's pawn, or existentialism.

*

> Goin down to Cripple Creek,
> Goin on the run,
> Goin down to Cripple Creek
> To have a little fun . . .

Though music has never been my main line of work, I have always kept some gig or another going on the side, found some combo to sit in with. I inherited this from him, of course, a connection so obvious it eluded me for half my life. I have played in dance bands and in piano bars, at New Years Eve parties and for weddings in June. I have played in total release sessions where anyone can get into the act, with any horn or rhythm-maker handy, to do whatever comes to mind.

For several years I spent half my mornings on classical and flamenco guitar. By that time he had pretty much quit playing. After the family moved down to Santa Clara Valley, his old picking buddies were too far away to meet with.

Most of them had packed up their instruments anyhow, when their fingers gave out. And by that time I was married, living here in Santa Cruz, starting my own family, taking on a few guitar students for the extra cash, and trying to go the distance with the classical repertoire—Villa-Lobos, Tarrega, Fernando Sor. Those days now stand for what pushed me farthest from him. Call it my own yearning for sophistication. I was never much good at sophistication. It runs right against the grain. But I confess that I have hungered for it. In the preludes and the nocturnes, I could taste it, and in the numerous baroque guitar suites I tried to master, in the Elizabethan galliards, in the Fantasía written by some 16th century lutenist whose three surviving works had recently been transcribed from nearly indecipherable tablatures.

I still love the galliards. I always will. But it took me twenty years of part-time music life to discover, or rather to quit being ashamed of the fact and come right out and admit that I love *San Antonio Rose* more. If I am sitting in a honky tonk when the pedal steel begins to whine the opening bars of that song, I have no choice but to surrender. I hear a calling in the blood. It launches me. It fills me with unabashed glee.

I can now trace this change in outlook to a bluegrass band I happened to join, during the very year dad passed away. At the time I told myself I was "between gigs," looking for new musical allies and looking for something I had not tried. But I am convinced that more than coincidence brought this group together. It was another version of the ancient maxim: when the musician is ready, the band will appear.

Everyone else had played a lot of country music. The mandolin picker was a graduate student from North Carolina. The banjo player came from Knoxville, Tennessee, by way of Viet Nam, discovering California like my dad did, passing through. I was the novice, and the first night we got together I was stupefied with boredom. One of the pleasures of playing string bass is working through a good set of chord changes, the challenging progression, the little surprise moves that have to be memorized. In bluegrass there are many tricky melodies to be executed by fiddle and banjo and mandolin, but no changes to speak of, three or four in most tunes, two in a lot of them, in some tunes no changes at all.

"Just hang on to that A minor, Jim baby!" the mandolin picker told me, as we began to play a modal breakdown featuring his shiny Gibson. "And for God sake, let me hear that A!"

It took some getting used to. It took a while to hear what was really going on with five stringed instruments, all acoustic, all made of wood. They wove a tapestry of sound, a tight braid of mountain counterpoint, and I found that I could squeeze inside the braid, pushing notes up from underneath for the fiddle and banjo to loop around. The best way to feel it is to stand in a circle, get moving on a song like *Blackberry Blossom* or *Cripple Creek*. Then all the strings and resonating chambers pulse at one another in intricate, skin-whiffling ways.

I told myself that bluegrass is rural chamber music, which, in a certain sense, is true. But those were mainly academic words I needed, to talk myself into it.

I soon discovered, or remembered, that my head was full of songs I had grown up hearing on "The Grand Ol Opry" out of Nashville. Dad used to listen to that show every Saturday night. I started taking vocals on some of Roy Acuff's great hits, *Wreck on The Highway*, *The Wabash Cannonball*. The other guys were bringing in truck driving songs, gospel numbers, old Jimmie Rodgers yodels, anything that tickled us, as long as we could call it "country," as long as we could do it acoustically and without piano and drums. We could afford to be purists because we all made our money other ways. We dressed up in boots and string ties and colored shirts and drank whiskey in the parking lot. I would often think of dad while we were playing, wishing he could have seen and heard all this, sometimes wondering why he had to pass away before I could embrace what I had resisted for so long.

I guess this band had been together for a couple of years when he finally turned up, very briefly, at a country fair outside of town.

There's a long low valley winding inland from the ocean and the coast road called Highway One. About five miles back, in a big open meadow, wooden booths had been nailed up out of rough-hewn planks and hung with flags and banners. The meadow was recently mowed. Hay was raked into mounds for picnickers to loll against. Steep stands of madrone and bay and redwood sloped away on both sides and seemed to gather all the sunlight into this grassy basin. It wasn't hot. Little breezes eddied through there all day long. But from noon on, the sun was so bright, the haystacks shimmered so, you could hardly look at them with the naked eye.

There were clay pots for sale, and embroidered shirts, and buffaloes of welded iron, and roasting corn, and ice cream, and free draft beer for the band, to chase down the Jim Beam we had stashed behind our sound system. By the end of the second set we were so loose we played *Foggy Mountain Breakdown* faster than we ever thought we could. Not one of us missed a note. We all agreed it was the best we had sounded. The scene had lifted us to its own excellence. And it was just then, as I stepped back into the shade, looking for a drink, high from the music, yet already wistful, afraid we might never be that good again, that I spotted him leaning against one of the hay bales, in between our bandstand and the curving line of booths.

He looked mighty comfortable, like this was how he had hoped to spend the day. His legs were stretched in front of him, ankles crossed, hands behind his head. He wore white shoes, white duck pants, a white shirt open at the collar, and a white, broad-brim plantation owner's hat, watching me carefully and almost smiling. He never had smiled much. Somehow it was difficult for him. He gave me as wide a smile as he'd ever been able to deliver, followed by his ultimate statement, that all-purpose sideways twist of the head, which in this case signified approval, and perhaps a hint of true delight. Then a strolling couple passed between us, and he was gone.

I stared at the hay mound until my eyes blurred, trying to conjure him up again and wishing to hell I had been born ten years before World War One, so we could have toured east Texas together, around 1928, when he first got back from Honolulu, out of the Navy and looking for some action. He and his pals had about twenty-five tunes between them and an old bathtub Model T. They hit all the towns between Fort Worth and Corpus Christi, actually played for a couple of months on a radio station out of Texarkana, two guitars and a country fiddle. He wore that white plantation owner's hat everywhere he went in those days, twenty-four years old at the time and a singing fool.

Initiation

Hell Week started with a gunny sack. "Cut out some arm holes," the pledgemaster told us, "so you can wear it under your shirt. And you better be damn sure you wear it under there all day every day and while you're in class, because a member could stop you any time anywhere."

The penalty, he said, would be more trouble than we'd care to get into. He was not specific about the penalty. He didn't have to be. He was not a man you wanted to push. He took a little too much pleasure in dreaming up tasks that would prove to the world how eager we were to join. He was also older than me by several years. Older than almost everyone, he should have been past the age where he needed to do this. He had already been to Korea and back. Maybe he had left too soon. Maybe he should have spent more time in the combat zone, getting certain things out of his system. And maybe we, his ten pledges, were the hostages he should have captured in another country, in some other campaign.

Now that I think of it, we were very much like prisoners of war. But that fall, which was the fall of 1952, I was not asking any questions. It was too late for questions. I had too much invested. In addition to the small penalty—that is, whatever the pledgemaster invented next, if I were

caught without my gunny sack—there was the larger penalty, which underscored each of his commands. Failure to
comply could mean rejection by the membership. Though
we had passed the first screening and been accepted as
pledges, we weren't members until we had made it
through a final ding session at the end of the Hell Week.
The vote had to be unanimous. One ding and you were
out. We had been pledging for a month, following orders
like this for a month. I was starting to feel like a survivor,
one who could go the distance. There were five days left
now, then Hell Night, and it would all be over.

That afternoon I happened to be sitting in a lecture hall,
waiting for my American History professor, and vaguely
hoping one of the members might appear out of nowhere
to spot-check my loyalty, when a beautiful young woman
asked me if I was all right.

I said, "Sure, I'm all right."

"You're squirming around so much. Do you have poi-
son oak or something?"

She had luscious black hair, tumbling past her shoulders, and exotic eyes, and I had been trying for two weeks
to get her attention. Now that I had it, I wanted to impress
her, come up with a remark that would give me stature.

I said, "I'm pledging a fraternity."

"Why are you squirming and scratching all the time?
You're making me nervous."

"It's this gunny sack."

I watched her glance behind me, above me, underneath
my seat, before she said, "What gunny sack?"

I pulled up my sweater and showed her the burlap
hairshirt with its potato-shipper logo.

She said, "Is this something religious?"

"I just have to wear it all week. It's a kind of test, I
guess."

She looked at me with alarm, then with pity, then she began to laugh. "You must be crazy. All week? You're going to get a bad skin rash."

I knew she felt sorry for me. And I felt sorry for her, sorry she did not grasp the meaning of my ordeal. This was her first quarter in college, whereas I was a sophomore transfer. I figured that might explain it: she was young. She was also Japanese. That was her background, and I thought that helped to explain why she was so far out of synch with the rhythms and demands of campus life. Some rigid Japanese attitude toward education. But this idea confused me, because she did not look rigid. She was radiant. Here was a radiant Asian woman sitting in this crowded lecture hall looking at me as if I were insane.

Loud footsteps interrupted us. The professor was striding toward his podium, in coat and tie. He was youthful, fiery, robust, a man who gestured wildly and took pride in startling his students. Without any introduction he opened a newspaper and read aloud from an inside page. He threw the paper onto the floor in disgust and told us we had just heard another half-truth from the lips of Tricky Dick.

He referred to Richard M. Nixon, who was then a thirty-nine year old Senator from California running for vice president on the Republican ticket behind Dwight D. Eisenhower. During that quarter we heard a lot about Tricky Dick, whom the youthful professor used as a kind of punctuation mark, whenever there was a point to make regarding some moment in American History he thought needed re-examining.

As he threw the paper down he launched into a lecture about the framers of the Constitution. "They have been called the Founding Fathers," he proclaimed. "I prefer to think of these fellows as the *Funding* Fathers. They were already in the habit of using slave labor to run their huge plantations. Do you think they designed a document that would jeopardize any of their holdings? I'm just asking you to think about why certain leaders do the things they do. You can be sure that if Tricky Dick gets elected, he will have more on his agenda than the best interests of the people who vote him into office . . ."

In those days these were risky opinions. Irreverence was out of fashion. The radical stance was out of fashion. Any form of rocking the boat was out of fashion. This professor was saying things I had never heard voiced in public. Even as I heard them I was only hearing words. Years would pass before the content kicked in, like a delayed-action booster rocket. Think of him now as a counterforce to the pledgemaster. If this were a morality play, the pledgemaster would be the implacable Chaplain of Machismo, while the professor would be the Prophet-Without-Portfolio, a distant voice, crying in the wilderness of the 1950s.

If this were a morality play, a third character would be the young woman sitting next to me. She was the only one who told me to my face that I might be crazy, the only one to raise so much as an eyebrow about what I thought I was doing. Later, after it was over and I realized she had been right, I found myself talking to her more and more. I could not stay away from her. Think of her as The Young Woman Who Is Sent As Guide.

*

It was the season for joining things. Everywhere else I turned that week I was admired or envied or in some way encouraged to proceed. I was taking a major step along the path toward fuller social life, and without social life how could there be any life at all? There were, in particular, dozens of young females for whom pledging was very much like going into battle. These were the dozens of so-

rority women who lived along The Row. They understood
exactly what was going on. In their eyes a pledge pin was
as good as a combat ribbon. Their approval, their looks
and touches, meant a lot to me. I was being admitted not
only into a club but into a larger community of men and
women who somehow recognized one another. By Hell
Week I had come to see myself the way these women did,
as a kind of soldier doing duty in the cause of comradeship
and righteous social life.

I was eighteen, in my second year of college, but new on
this campus, and three fraternities had invited me to rush
parties. It was heady stuff. Each club's name took the form
of Greek letters, which seemed to signify something large,
something traditional and learned, yet mysterious in an almost alchemical way, and also "national." The members
like to use the word "national" to re-enforce a claim or a
theory about their club. "So-and-so is coming out from national in a couple of weeks."

At the rush parties there were kegs of beer, plates of fried
chicken at an outdoor Italian restaurant on the edge of
town, with smoker movies to follow, old scratchy black-
and-white footage of the French housemaid in her skimpy
apron submitting first to the chauffeur, then to the smirk-
ing husband in his lounging jacket and finally to the wife.
All this seemed manly and worldly, the kind of thing one
ought to be doing in college. The members belonged to a
local "chapter," and they called themselves "brothers,"
and that too felt good. I had never had any brothers. Many
of them wore shirts that made them look mature, shirts
with button-down collars, and chinos, and white-buck
shoes. And they already seemed to have access to those
women across the street, in their pleated skirts, their cash-
mere sweaters with the raglan sleeves.

The club I chose to pledge included one fellow I had

known in highschool, a talented miler, now majoring in biology. Having nominated me, he took me under his wing. I will call him The Confidant. He is a fourth character in this drama. He was among those who had discovered the glamorizing effect of pinstripe shirts with button-down collar, and white buck shoes. He looked seasoned to me now, a veteran of something. Since he was older than me by about six months, he called me "kid."

"Hey kid," he would say, "did it ever occur to you that there are only two kinds of sorority girls—onions, and popsicles?"

He could deliver a line like that, and the question itself would make you laugh. We would both start laughing, and it didn't matter if there was an answer.

"Your onion," he would say, "brings tears to your eyes every time you look at her. But your popsicle, the more you lick her the sweeter and softer she gets."

During Hell Week he became my mentor, a coach advising me on how to prevail. When the gunny sack began to chafe and burn, he told me, "Use cornstarch down inside. Anybody complains, tell em it's a doctor's prescription. Tell em they're welcome to call your dermatologist."

When they started keeping us up all night, waxing floors in the fraternity house, and scrubbing out toilets, he said, "Take cat naps whenever you can. Take turns with the other guys. Cover for each other. Save your strength for the weekend."

On Hell night his final words to me were, "If they make you chew tobacco, don't swallow any more than you have to. That is what makes you sick. The main thing is stay cool. It's almost over, kid." He repeated that, with what I took to be a meaningful and fatherly look. "It's almost over."

We had been told to wear worthless clothes, "something

you can throw away later," the pledgemaster said. As we assembled in the front room, awaiting further instructions, we looked like a work crew. The fact is, we *were* a work crew. We had moved furniture, clearing this room of its rugs and lamps and upholstered chairs. We had mowed lawns, swept a chimney, hauled rubbish. We had already put in a full day, and now the pledgemaster was unwrapping plugs of dark tobacco.

"Don't be afraid to break off a big piece," he said, with a grin. He too was dressed for rough travel—jeans, fatigue jacket, combat boots. He had been drinking beer all afternoon, along with most of the members. They were trickling in, gathering to watch the action.

"I don't want to see any spitting either. Chew it a while, then swallow a while, then chew a while, and so forth."

None of us, I learned later, had chewed tobacco before that night. None of us, of course, would admit this. We dutifully broke off chaws and started grinding our teeth. I kept my head down, trying to fake it, holding the chaw under my tongue. Others, being more obedient, soon turned green.

"Now we're going to try some jumping jacks," the pledgemaster said. "In unison. And look sharp. We'll do it by the numbers."

To his military count we began to jump, legs wide, arms high, while members chimed in, "Hut two! Hut two! Hut two! Hut two!"

The jumping jacks didn't last long. The fellow next to me vomitted across the wooden floor, an astonishing geyser that drew loud applause. I was appointed to help him clean up the mess—my punishment for half-hearted and devious chewing. The reek of it pushed me to the edge of nausea. I was thankful to be herded outside, where the breathing was easier.

The next event was a two-lap sprint around the block, during which we had to continue chewing and display the chaw at the finish line. This was a good-size block, perhaps a quarter-mile circuit. The last one in would have to run a third lap, and for sluggards there could perhaps be other penalties. So it became a half-mile race, at the end of which four more pledges vomitted into the shrubbery, along with the fellow who had vomitted inside, sick again from the fresh chaw the pledgemaster had provided.

I was queasy, but still not sick, having held most of my saliva til I hit a dark stretch of sidewalk, splatting it out onto someone's lawn. If I'd had a few minutes after the race, my stomach might have settled down. But now quarts of warm beer were waiting. There was going to be a chug-a-lug contest. In the stripped front room, members ganged around again, drinking with us, rooting wildly, while the pledgemaster warned, "I don't want to see any more puking. No spitting. No puking. No peeing. Everybody got that?"

We drank, we gulped, we spilled, and then we were told to take everything off.

"Down to your underwear," the pledgemaster said.

You could see he was making it up as he went along. He had envisioned the ten of us crammed into one hardwood corner.

"These are your pledge brothers," he said. "I just want you fellows to get better acquainted. So get *close* to each other."

We thought he meant pack in tight like a crowded elevator. He wanted a pile of bodies like a goal-line stand. Other members approved of this. Shouts came at us from around the room.

"Hey, get close to each other!"

"You guys aren't getting close enough!"

"Are we talking about brotherhood or what? Squeeze in there!"

We squeezed and pushed ourselves into a sweaty, naked tangle of arms and legs and mouths that reeked of vomit breath and tobacco juice and beer, which finally broke apart when one of the fellows on the bottom began to retch and cry out for air and mercy. Unscrambling, we put our clothes on, and they sent us outdoors for another two laps around the block.

It wasn't a race this time, since there was obviously nothing to be won. There was only endurance, which meant conserving energy. We took our time, spreading out. Around the second corner I stopped to rest and to confer with a fellow pledge slumped against a tree. He too was eighteen, from Palo Alto, where his father owned a dry cleaners. He was despondent.

I said, "You okay?"

"Almost."

"Breathe deep."

"It's not that."

"What's the matter?"

"I'm not going back."

"You have to."

"That's my car across the street. I'm just going to get in it and drive home. This is all too chickenshit."

"You can't quit now."

"It's infantile," he said.

"Couple of hours. That's all we have left."

"They're going to ding me anyhow. I know it."

"Hey, nobody's going to get dinged," I said. "After all this crap they've put us through? They would have dinged us a month ago, if they were going to. C'mon."

When I had jogged a few more yards, I could hear his footsteps, at a slow run. The sound depressed me. I guess I wanted him to bolt. If he had, I might have gone with him. Suddenly I was overwhelmed by the absurdity of this night. The guzzled beer had given me a headache. My weariness had turned to stupefying fatigue.

Back at the house everyone's mood had shifted. Most of the members had disappeared. We were being lined up for the final interview, the so-called moment of truth and point of no return, the nature of which was shrouded in mystery. All I knew was that it occurred in a curtained room on the ground floor, and we went in one at a time, and we were kept apart until the ritual ended.

When my turn came I was ushered into a half-dark chamber, lit with candles, where the brotherhood had assembled, forty or fifty fellows seated at tables, watching me. The beer-drinking hilarity had somehow subsided. Told to stand in front of them, I felt vulnerable and on display, acutely conscious of my disheveled clothes, which smelled of sweat and someone else's vomit. I don't remember all that was said. What I remember is the monastic feeling, everything formal, and semi-lit, with the faces of the brotherhood in shadow and in yellow candle flame. I heard the words "chapter" and "national," and then came the crucial question.

"Does any member feel this pledge should not be admitted to our fraternity?"

During the brief silence no one moved. I was waiting yet not waiting. After five nights of almost no sleep I was giddy with exhaustion, still this side of nausea. Having just endured the last hour I thought I had jumped through the final hoop. I found myself poised on the threshold of recklessness. A little arrogance was creeping in. I could take their club or leave it alone.

A chair scraped. I looked around. It was my Confidant, coming to his feet in the middle of this roomful of silent men. With a very serious face he said, "I have to cast a vote against him. I've been watching him this month. I just don't think he qualifies."

There was no smile, no hint this might be a joke. No one in the room was smiling, or moving. They had the look of inquisitors now, and my Confidant had the face of a demon, lit from below by the nearest candle, shadowed, and harsh. His words were devastating. I stood there blinking, looking at him. I almost fell to the floor. Much later I saw how the whole week had brought me to a kind of breaking point. Five days of low-grade humiliation, five sleepless nights. It is like brain-washing. It bends you. It wears you down. If this was comedy, I had lost my sense of humor. If this was real, I had no resources for confronting it.

"Goddam you!" I shouted, bolting for the door. "Goddam all you sonsabitches!"

Running blind I headed toward the street, but a hedge stopped me. I turned to the closest wall and drove a fist into it three or four times. The wall happened to be stucco. It tore my knuckles open. That seemed to impress the two brothers who were right behind me. The sight of ragged skin and flowing blood was a sign of something, a sign of how much their club meant to me.

"Hey, take it easy," one of them called.

"Get the hell away from me!"

"Hey, listen, man. He didn't mean it."

I turned on him, ready to punch. "If I'm out, I'm out! Forget it! Go fuck yourselves!"

He grabbed my arm. "Will you listen to me? You're not out."

"What do you mean?"

"I mean, he didn't mean it. It was a little, I dunno, a . . . You know. The final step. That's all."

"He didn't mean it?"

"He was just kidding. Believe me. You think he'd vote against you?"

"But he did. I heard him."

I was disoriented now, without strength or will.

"C'mon," they said, "relax. Relax."

"I don't get it," I said. "I don't get it."

They bandaged my hand, then they blindfolded me and led me to a waiting car. All ten of us were blindfolded. We were caravanning somewhere. No one had been dinged. It had all been theatre. Much later I learned that each of us had received the same treatment—a staged denouncement from the brother we felt closest to.

I don't know how long we drove. I had a vague sense of rising curves. I was dozing, weak from the adrenalin rush and then the sudden draining away of rage. I no longer cared what happened, as long it moved this endless night toward some completion.

I may have dreamed of The Young Woman Sent As Guide, walking with me through an open field, through a field of bright flowers, under a dazzling sky. Or perhaps I heard the dream voice of The Prophet-Without-Portfolio, whispering unheeded warnings, although I doubt it. I don't remember dreaming. If this were all being staged, and if there were rear-screen projectors, those two faces would be high up on the cyclorama, much larger than life and observing the action from above. On that same cyclorama there would be a third face, indistinct, the flash-forward of a character we do not meet until the final scenes.

*

I don't remember waking up. I remember being led from the car into what felt like a clearing, still blindfolded. We were outdoors. It was colder. The air felt thinner. There were many voices, loud voices of raucous greeting. I heard fire crackling. I felt the soreness in my bandaged hand, the sting of the wound, the swelling. I could smell beer, and I wouldn't have minded a bottle just then. The dozing had eased my stomach. My mouth was cotton dry.

The pledgemaster's voice cut through the swirl of wisecracks and mock-commands. "I know you fellows are thirsty after that ride. So line it up here. Everybody get in a good straight line."

"These rascals are thirsty," someone said.

"You *know* they're thirsty," said someone else.

"Well, be a brother and give em something to drink."

"How about a brew? I don't want to have to haul any of this horsepiss back down to town."

"They deserve something better than beer, don't you think?"

"Will you assholes shut up a minute," the pledgemaster said. "I've got it right here. Just what the doctor ordered. Open wide now," he told us, "and don't complain, and don't spit anything out. You have to swallow it."

Though I could not see him at the time, I see him now, in his jeans and his olive-drab G.I. jacket, moving along our blind-folded rank in the firelight, a fatigue-jacket priest delivering unholy eucharist to our waiting lips. I was fourth. Before he reached me I could hear gagging and choking. And yet I stood there with my mouth open. I am still amazed by the willingness of that surrender.

The shock of expulsion had drained me. In the aftermath, all my resistance dissolved. I was weak with relief, glad to know I remained among the chosen—though more than membership was now at stake. If I refused his as-yet-unidentified beverage, I would be letting down my fellow pledges. We had come this far together. I must endure what they were enduring. At the same time, though others had gagged and choked, perhaps I would not. Perhaps I could take it, whatever *it* was, and thus prove something. But prove it to whom? To myself? To these drunks careening back and forth across the clearing? To the sadistic pledgemaster, The Chaplain of Machismo, who had a way of making everything a test of manliness?

"Here ya go," he said, as a slick bottle touched my mouth. "Down the hatch."

It was cheap salad oil, thick and nearly rancid. I did not want to gag. I tried to swallow, felt my stomach lurch. He kept pouring until it ran down my chin and onto my shirt. I swallowed again, let it spill, then listened to the efforts of the fellow next in line, and waited for the second course, raw fish, chunks of slippery cod we had to swallow whole. They lodged in the throat like a second tongue. I remember raw and salted oysters, and molasses, great spoonfuls of blackstrap molasses. Other members joined in for this. Some fed us. Some moved along behind our rank with jars of syrup and boxes of Cornflakes, anointing us.

When the blindfolds came off at last, my eyes went first to the bonfire, popping with sparks that rose into the starry night, then to the orange faces around the clearing, and the grills of cars and pickups among the trees. I searched for my Confidant, thought I spotted him near the stacked cases of beer. I guess I wanted some sign from him, a signal of reassurance. I couldn't catch his eye. The flames made moving shadows everywhere, and I was blinking back syrup. I looked right and left at my fellow pledges, who were looking at me. We all had to laugh. We were fellow clowns in dripping clothes, our faces oiled, our heads shampooed with Cornflakes. These were sickly and reluctant laughs, as we waited to see what came next, hoping it was over, knowing it wasn't, knowing the worst was yet to come.

"Five of you guys stay right where you are," the pledgemaster said. "You other five come over here."

He stood in front of a fifty-gallon barrel. While he spoke, another member, who happened to be a famous linebacker that season, unzipped his fly and began to pee into the barrel. To clear the rim, he had to stand on a case of beer.

The pledgemaster was furious. "What do you think you're doing?" he cried.

The linebacker said, "What does it look like I'm doing?"

"You can't pee in there!"

"Why the hell not?"

The pledgemaster looked around the clearing as if someone had just stolen the keys to his car. "Goddam it! Goddam it to hell! I can't believe this!"

A tumult arose, a confusion of yelling and joking, orders and counter-orders. This drunken linebacker, it turned out, had saved us from a slimy fate. Earlier that day two of my pledge brothers had been sent in a pickup truck out to the pasturelands beyond the town, to fill this barrel with cow manure. It had been hauled up here to provide the evening's finale. Five of us were to stand on one side of the barrel, while the other five hurled manure in gobs and handfuls. You wonder who would have had the worst of it, the hurlers or the hurlees.

We never found out. The pledgemaster decided this linebacker's urine had somehow defiled the barrel and spoiled the plan. He was ready to trade blows.

"You really are a stupid sonofabitch!" the pledgemaster yelled.

"What the fuck difference does it make?" the linebacker said.

"You ruined it, that's all! You just ruined it!"

The argument was so preposterous, it occurs to me now that this too may have been staged—like the ding session—in order to make us cringe one more time with perverse gratitude. But I doubt it. The effect would hardly have been worth hauling a fifty-gallon barrel of very wet manure that far into the mountains. It was exactly the kind of main event our pledgemaster would have imagined, and now he was making excellent use of his disappointment. He blamed the linebacker for pushing him farther than he might ordinarily have gone, forcing him to come up with a new finale.

There is an aromatic liniment called oil of wintergreen, sometimes applied to painful knees and elbows and shoulders. You have to use it sparingly and with care because it can sting and burn. The one place you do not want any to fall is on the genitals.

Our last instructions were to drop our pants and then our shorts. Again, it amazes me, looking back, that we willingly stood there while various members doused our private parts with this ointment that causes your crotch to scream and your balls to shrivel as if held over glowing coals.

While we howled and bellowed, the remaining beer was thrown into cars, cold engines roared to life, and the entire membership drove away, leaving us on a mountaintop, staggering around the dwindling campfire. When we discovered that standing still hurt more than moving, we headed out to the road and began our slow, agonized descent. Oil of wintergreen is said to relieve the effects of acute rheumatism, but in our case it worked the opposite way, creating a band of bowlegged, hobbling cripples.

It was then about 3 a.m. It might have been an hour later when a local rancher, up early, happened to drive by and take pity and let us pile onto his flatbed, haggard and moaning.

*

Now it is time for those faces up there on the cyclorama to grow brighter, the faces that quietly kept watch over Hell Night—The Prophet-Without-Portfolio, and The Young Woman Sent As Guide, and the half-seen profile, who turns out to be the young woman's father. I only met him once, and on that occasion he would not speak to me. If this were a morality play, he would be The Sphinx Elder, the One Who Remains Silent, yet seems to know everything.

Before I met him, of course, I had to get better acquainted with the young woman. And before that could happen I had to return to my American History class, which I postponed for several days, while I gave myself a short vacation, to lick my wounds, and to do some overdue work on my car. During this interval, Dwight D. Eisenhower had defeated Adlai Stevenson for the presidency, in a landslide victory that did not surprise the youthful professor.

I have a vivid memory of his response to that election. He stood in front of us, as if he himself were a candidate for office, and said, "Ladies and gentlemen, if you remember anything at all from this course, please remember what I am about to say! Richard Nixon is the most dangerous man in the United States!"

In the fall of 1952 this meant almost nothing to me. It was his fervor that endured. He had the voice and the delivery of a gospel minister. The remark stayed alive somewhere in my mind, not because I understood it, but because of how he said it, and because of something else that happened soon afterward, as if his passion had awakened other passions waiting to be expressed.

The young woman with the radiant face and the Asian eyes was seated next to me again and watching me with a large smile I took to be friendly. When the lecture ended she did not mention it or the election or any other feature of American history past or present. Neither one of us had been listening very carefully. The fact is, eight years would pass before we talked about what we had just heard. The professor's bold remark would lie dormant until Nixon's first presidential campaign, against John F. Kennedy.

As we lingered in the classroom she said, "You're not squirming around so much. I guess you're in the fraternity now."

I said, "That's right."

"What happened to your hand?"

I held it up, still bandaged, and looked at it and considered inventing an answer that sounded brave. Something in her eyes said she wanted a real answer, not a clever one. I found myself describing what had happened at the ding session, surprised at how good it felt to be able to talk about this. We walked out of the building together, with me talking. When I stopped, when I reached the part about the stucco wall, she said, "Why are people so cruel to one another?"

I was stunned. The word *cruel* would never have occurred to me. Yet as soon as she said it, I saw that she was right. The sincerity of her question told me she understood everything I had just said, plus a great deal more. And she had asked it as if I might actually know the answer. Though I didn't, I felt more knowledgeable. I felt older in her presence, both older and younger. I began to melt inside. I see now that I had reached a point where I wanted all my preconceptions and misconceptions to be challenged, but I did not even know where to begin. I think I felt she might lead me somewhere I had not been and needed to go. She was both innocent and wise, and that was the day I fell for her, as we walked across the campus talking about joining and belonging.

I did not yet know that one of the small cruelties she had already absorbed was the fact that she would never be considered for membership in a Greek-letter club with national affiliations, not as a Japanese American, back in 1952. As we began to spend more and more time together, this gradually sank in. I began to see The Row through her eyes, as a realm she could not enter, except as a kind of tourist on a weekend visa, that is, as my partner at a Friday night dance.

It was toward the end of fall quarter that I found myself driving along a country road looking for her house. We were going somewhere on a Saturday afternoon, and she had said she could meet me in town, but I insisted on picking her up.

The house was set back from the road, among outbuildings, at the edge of a recently cultivated field. Her father was working strawberries then. As I pulled into the yard he appeared on the porch, in his jeans and his old felt hat. I was driving my 1938 Chevy sedan. He looked first at the car, with grave doubt, and then at me. He had a thin, black moustache, and a lean, weathered, aristocratic face.

When I told him my name and said I was there to pick up his daughter, he shook his head and seemed to cough. He stepped down off the porch and stood with his feet planted and his hands on his hips, holding me with his eyes in a way that forced me to look at him.

In that brief exchange, at the edge of his forty acres of strawberry furrows, I saw a man, or felt the spirit of a kind of man previously unknown to me, a man from Asia, from Japan, a man who, I would later learn, had lost relatives in the bombing of Hiroshima. Thirty years before I was born he had immigrated to the United States, to work, to live. His home region was in a deep depression when he left, at age seventeen, on a steamship bound for The Land of

Promise. After the attack on Pearl Harbor he was arrested and charged with being an enemy spy, and he lost a career while sitting out the war in an internment camp called Manzanar, in eastern California. He was so scarred by that experience, he had stopped speaking to Caucasians. It was a point of honor. Now, into the front yard had come a sun-tanned, anglo frat-house fledgling with scales on his eyes and lust in his heart, driving a neglected '38 Chevy and looking for the daughter, the youngest of ten children and the first to go away to college.

All this was in his face. Though I could not have known it, I must have felt it. I felt something coming from him, and it was not hatred. What he projected was the hard-won toughness of a man who had survived everything America and Japan had thrown at him, and who had found a way to continue.

For me it was a moment of awakening. A window had been opened, for the first small glimpse of another world, I should say another way of seeing the white American world I had grown up to take for granted.

*

I cannot honestly say I quit the fraternity in order to take some kind of stand against discrimination. But that doubt, fueled by my affection for the young woman, released other doubts. I began to mutter and grumble around the house and find fault and ask questions that made certain members uneasy.

One day I asked the chairman of the membership committee if we ever pledged non-Caucasians. He was a junior, twenty years old, from Lodi. He said if it were up to him there would be no problem at all. But policies had been established back at national. "Not long ago," he said with knitted brow, "one chapter challenged the policy and got suspended. I mean it is still something they are looking at very closely."

On the day I told my Confidant I was thinking about quitting, he said, "You can't."

I said, "Why not?"

"You have to talk it over with the president and the treasurer. They are the only ones who can make a decision like that."

"You mean I can't decide for myself?"

"You'll have to talk to them," he said.

So I met with these two in the chapter office and announced I was planning to quit.

"What's your reason?" said the treasurer.

"Do I have to give you a reason? I just don't want to belong any more."

"Is it the dues?"

"Maybe I owe for one more month."

"If it's the dues, we could give you a grace period or something."

"It's not the dues."

"His reason isn't the issue anyway," the president said. "He *can't* quit."

"Why not?" I asked.

"It's a policy set back at national," the president said, as if this settled the matter.

"What's the policy?" I said.

"Nobody can quit the fraternity until he has been a fulltime dues-paying member for at least two years."

"And according to our records," said the treasurer, with the maddening precision that would make him a top CPA later in life, "you have only been paying dues here for three months."

"Well," I said, "I don't think that policy applies to me."

"What are you talking about?" the president said hotly.

"It only applies to fraternity members. Right?" As they both nodded, I continued. "So it doesn't apply to me, because I don't belong to the fraternity any more. I have just handed in my resignation."

Thanks to the quality of argument and debate in that community back then, my logic carried the day. I walked out the door a free man, and stepped directly into the arms of The Young Woman Who Had Been Sent As Guide. She was waiting around the corner in my sedan. A few years later we were married, and she is still surprising me with questions that cannot be dismissed. Just this morning she said, "Do you ever feel like you are a director filming a movie of your life?"

*

If this were the movie version of a morality play, we would now be seeing headshots of the other figures, with quick summaries of how they ended up.

THE CHAPLAIN OF MACHISMO: He re-enlisted.

THE SPHINX ELDER: The day our paths crossed, he was already 65. Not long afterward he passed away.

THE PROPHET-WITHOUT-PORTFOLIO: He was a man ahead of his time. He should have started teaching in the 1960s instead of in the 1950s. At the end of that academic year he was fired. A boat-rocker. He moved on, to other jobs on other campuses and I lost track of him. But the great wheel turned, and he re-entered our lives, more than twenty years after The Young Woman and I had first sat side by side in his classroom. It seemed to complete some kind of cycle, also to begin a new one. He had not changed much. He was still prophesying. This was about the time Nixon had resigned the presidency, midway through his second term, in order to evade impeachment proceedings. "He should be locked up," the Prophet said.

"But he won't be. You mark my words. Ten or twelve years from now, Tricky Dick will be back in the limelight. He will be on the cover of TIME. Or NEWSWEEK. Or both!"

THE CONFIDANT: I had to forgive him twice. The first time was easy. During the days after Hell Week I was so swept away by the comraderie that greeted our safe return from the high country, I welcomed every back slap and round of beer and handshake that came my way, including his. One of the boys at last, I was full of brotherly feeling toward them all. But The Young Woman had given me another way to think about the ding session, and it niggled me for years, as I wondered from time to time how someone who called himself a brother and a friend could take part in a ritual so degrading. One to one, I knew, he would never have been capable of that. Context was the key, I told myself. A group can always call out things the individual might otherwise hold in check. Accepting this, I was able to forgive him a second time, though it has kept me wary of clubs in general and committees of every kind. I was never much of joiner anyway.

The Window Of War

It was during the Lebanon crisis, an earlier one, the Lebanon crisis of 1958. Every American aircraft in Europe stood at the ready. With no war on we milked any crisis or incident or exercise that came along. Troops were being flown from Germany down to the Aegean. Tactical squadrons were ferrying over from the states. I remember one story, and this is just an aside, about a flight of four ferry planes, F-100s, crossing the Atlantic, when the lead pilot started hallucinating. His heating system had jammed at full. He was dehydrating. He thought he saw an airfield below him. He saw the runway and the control tower, and there was nothing any of his flying mates could do. He simply peeled off for a landing and went in.

Pilots liked to tell such stories. They circulated quickly around an airbase, throughout a command. Each man told it as if he'd been flying in the next plane. Pilots grew animated when they told crash stories, their flat hands swerving, plunging. These stories always ended with the same line. "He bought the farm. He bought the goddam farm."

I didn't repeat them because I was not a pilot. To hear such stories I had to get them second-hand from the sergeant in my office or by eavesdropping at the club. Pilots

63

seldom told crash stories to non-flying officers, as if to say, "You wouldn't understand. You don't know what it's like up there."

They were right. I didn't know, and I didn't particularly want to know. The less I knew the better.

I lived offbase at the time, in a small thatch-roof cottage about four hundred years old. Some mornings, lying in bed, staring up at dark oak beams, or looking through leaded windows out onto a yellow Essex wheatfield, I could forget the planes parked beyond the first rise, forget I was in the Air Force at all. I could be the Great American Wanderer, having found at last the yeoman's Tudor cottage of my dreams. At twilight I could pursue this fantasy, or at sunrise, hiking a misty back road past blocks of thatched cottages like my own, past the Guild Hall, seat of public meetings for five centuries, past The Fox and Hounds, the village green. This was England, durable, dependable, each house the secure domain of some old-world craftsman—until nine each morning, when our F-100s began to blast off, roaring up and over the fields, over the Guild Hall, gushing tail flame.

The morning Lebanon came along I was waking slowly, watching murky fields in the half-light of a winter dawn, thinking of nothing, floating somewhere out on the screen of mist, when the siren started to rise like the howl of an abandoned dog. It rose and peaked and fell to a growl and climbed again, and my chest went hollow. I looked at the clock. 5:05. I'd have to be on base in twenty minutes. I didn't want to go. I wanted someone to call and tell me I didn't have to be there. I wanted the Wing Commander to call me personally and say it was all right, take your time, enjoy your breakfast, come in at ten.

Downstairs the phone jangled. As I sprang from the bed's warmth into the ice rink of my hallway, I knew this was not the Wing Commander. It was my network call. Most of us lived offbase, hooked together by a telephone grid, so that every man, even those in distant villages beyond the long reach of the siren, could get word within ten minutes after it blew. This was the theory. The network seldom worked. Someone was always away on leave or had moved and changed a number or was too hungover to respond. The local county switchboard, where all these calls had to intersect, sometimes collapsed under the sudden load. On other mornings I had listened to the siren's lonely rise and fall, waiting for a call that did not make it through, giving me then the perfect alibi. But today my contact man was right on schedule.

His voice barked, "Houston?"

"Yeah, this is Houston."

"You hear that siren?"

"What siren?"

"We got a Red Alert, fella."

There were three kinds, Red, Yellow and Blue. My contact, Major Walt Larkin, believed in all three. He was a career man who believed in everything he did, or claimed to.

I said, "Why Red? What's the matter?"

"Probably this Lebanon thing. I'll see ya down at the shack."

He referred to the gray shell of a quonset hut on the far side of the runway, where twenty-five of us, non-flying officers and NCO's, assembled during alerts. On normal duty we had low priority jobs—personnel, commissary, special services, building and grounds. When the siren rose, all such work was cut to a minimum or suspended, while each man reported to his combat duty station. Major Larkin and I and the others bunched into the shack became Couriers, charged with transferring nuclear warheads from the ammunition dump to the flight line. Like everyone else, I had made practice runs, but I had not yet seen an actual warhead, nor did I expect to see one. We practiced with pickup trucks and empty wooden cages called *dummies,* and somehow that seemed fitting. In my view that was about as much as we deserved to be entrusted with.

The shack was cold and furnished with metal chairs, and on those damp and sunless mornings when you needed caffeine most, the coffee arrived late, going first to flight-line crews and pilots and maintenance people and base-operations staff and bombing officers and the Wing Commander and anyone else who had something to do with planes. After the coffee urn was plugged in and I'd had my first sip I could begin to see this scene as parody. There we were, shivering in a convex meat locker, sitting on our folding chairs, in steel helmets, with canteens around our waists, slung from web belts, .45s in our holsters, two dozen second-stringers trying to look as tough and seasoned as Aldo Ray in *The Naked and The Dead.*

Usually I sat off in a corner and read the paper, hoping my name would not be called. Larkin was our commander, a small, slender, meticulous man, good at paperwork, but not a born leader. He knew the location and status of every piece of paper in the Wing Personnel office, where he was Deputy Chief. Out there in the shack, where he was Senior Courier, he spent most of his time trying not to be frightened. I frightened him, I knew. Whenever he looked at me I glowered like a general, and his eyes would grow wide with confusion. As a result I had made only three courier runs during my twenty months at the base, although we'd had seven alerts. I had one year left to serve, maybe less, if I could engineer an early discharge. If I could continue to intimidate Larkin maybe my name would never be called again, and I would set a record for Courier Neglect.

That is how I saw it at the time, as an extended prank,

awarding myself private points after each little exchange with the major. The truth was, I played hard-to-get with Larkin because I too was afraid. I was afraid to get involved. Somehow I believed it was possible to spend three years on active duty and not participate in the military's mission, its endless preparations for the unthinkable war. I was twenty-four and had come of age in 1950s California, in a time and a place of relative calm, barely acknowledging what happened in Korea, bluffing my way through ROTC as a strategy for sidestepping the draft. Then, in the course of one summer, after nine weeks of indoctrination in Texas, at Lackland Air Force Base, I found myself to be an Information Officer on active duty overseas, assigned to a Tactical Fighter-Bomber Wing where pilots were leaking stories of their Iron Curtain target plans, and sirens could come howling at you through the misty English dawn.

I have to confess something here, since it is part of the story, and it is something I could never have admitted to myself at the time: I loved the uniforms. At Lackland we drilled a lot. Under the cloudless Texas sky I had seen my profile on the parade ground asphalt—hat squared, sharp visor, khaki crease. In my memory it is stamped there, one profile in a long row thrown by forty young lieutenants. At such moments I stood with all the patriots I'd been seeing on recruiting posters since 1942, the stiff saluters gazing skyward. I was one with the rugged, joking, hard-eyed movie warriors who had fought well and held tight everywhere from North Africa to Normandy. I enjoyed my uniforms almost as much as Major Larkin did. This is why I scorned him. He was too familiar.

When he called my name I pretended not to hear, holding high my copy of the *Daily Telegraph*.

He raised his voice. "Lieutenant Houston!"

I rustled the paper then lowered it until he could see my hostile eyes peering above the headlines. Seeing his eyes widen I thought I had him once again. But this time he held.

"Take Sergeant Cairns and Sergeant Perez here and report to Special Weapons Area, building five, for transferral of weapons."

As if insulted beyond forgiveness I carefully folded the *Telegraph,* shoved it inside my wooly winter shirt, buttoned my topcoat, and led the sergeants outside to a waiting pickup. The motorpool driver had his orders. The engine was warm. We climbed in back. In five minutes we reached the high wire fence around the ammo area. We all showed security passes. Mine was stamped TOP SECRET, though the number of secrets revealed to me so far would not have altered the history of western civilization by very much.

Inside the fence we stopped at a long, grass-covered mound, a bunker built by the RAF during World War Two, now used to house our bombs. Another lieutenant stood by its metal door. I knew him. We sometimes drank beer at the club. His name was Mel Brown. Out here at the ammo dump he was no longer Mel. He wore a big ID card on his wool shirt, with a post-office mug shot. His thin blond hair was a web of wisps and tangled strands. His face was masking something. In the stark light from a lamp over the doorway he looked like a man who had just been told he has a terminal disease.

Our driver backed to the door. He and Mel lifted into the rear a wooden cage that housed a metal cartridge about six inches in diameter and maybe six inches high. This was not a dummy. For reasons unexplained to us, it was the real thing. Now our job was to deliver it to a hardstand, where it would be attached to a fighter-bomber that might well be aimed at Leningrad. I had to sign for it.

I glanced inside the truck. Cairns and Perez sat side by side, balancing carbines in their laps, each clutching a corner of the cage, their eyes pinched with awe and dread. I had thought they were hardened professionals. They had the rugged G.I. look of soldiers who could be relied on for foxhole survival or beachhead invasions anywhere, Sicily, Guadalcanal. Cairns, in fact, had waded ashore in one or two such campaigns. Now he was thirty-four, with five years between him and an early retirement. I had admired Cairns, from a distance. His handsome features were eroded by creases that seemed honorably earned, like German fencing scars. When I saw this face show naked alarm, it unnerved me. Obviously none of us had ever handled more than a dummy.

I glanced again at Mel Brown. Was he trembling? Was he on the verge of tears? Later I learned he had arrived on base that morning without the key to the ammo building, and his superior, Major Clive Morton, had recently misplaced the other key. Thus, while the rest of Europe readied for yet another apocalyptic showdown, our Wing, with its seventy-five supersonic fighter-bombers and its ten dozen supersonic pilots, had come to a temporary standstill waiting for Mel Brown to drive back home in search of his key.

At the time I didn't know this. The crazed look in his young eyes just added to my mounting uneasiness. On his clipboard I signed my name, then climbed back in, next to the warhead that was now my responsibility.

As leader of this patrol I held two corners of the cage, while Cairns and Perez held a corner each. Our aim was to keep it from jiggling. Brown had assured us there was no danger of detonation until some safety device had been triggered. I didn't believe him. Neither did the sergeants. Cairns managed to say, "That little gadget's worth about twenty-five thousand dollars, did you know that, lootenant?"

Somehow this detail hit harder than the fact of the bomb itself. I had never personally been liable for anything that expensive. I sat there staring at my obligation.

In those days it was a closely guarded secret that our planes in England carried nuclear devices. At least we told ourselves this secret was being closely guarded. As Information Officer I had hedged the point a hundred times, at community meetings, in news conferences, on long-distance calls from London journalists.

"Yes, that's correct," I would say, "our planes do have a nuclear capability."

"And do you have nuclear weapons right there on the base?"

"Sorry. Can't answer yes or no to that one."

"A number of our readers are concerned, you know, about the presence of these devices on British soil."

"We fully understand that. I can assure you we aren't doing anything that would endanger the local population."

"But if your planes have a nuclear capability, leftenant, surely the weapons will be close at hand. Otherwise you'd have a different aircraft out there. I mean, it would be rather silly to have a plane one could not exploit to the fullest, wouldn't it, leftenant."

"I should probably remind you," I would say, "that they still perform extremely well with conventional weapons . . ."

It was a game we played, the reporters and I. Since I had never seen a nuclear device with my own eyes, I could play it convincingly. It is easy to do when you have only seen the planes and not their secret cargo. When there is no war on, and you only see the take-offs and the landings, it is easy to marvel at the sleek power and the silvery thrust. Sometimes, as I watched a pair of them rise over the wheatfields across the road from my cottage, I could admire the thrilling spectacle and let the noise itself, the overwhelming thunder, bury all thought of the battles they were preparing for. At such times I almost believed my own releases. Perhaps, went my silent rationale, we really don't have the warheads out here. Such noble birds as these couldn't actually be loaded.

Now I was holding it in my hands, between my knees, my country's hope and grim salvation, freighted with all the nightmare imagery it had accumulated since 1945: mile-wide pits in the Nevada desert, Pacific atolls obliterated, Hiroshima, Nagasaki, radiation sores that never heal. These little canisters had raised the stakes of war so high that starting one seemed suicidal for all concerned. And yet by afternoon this one could be falling from the sky somewhere over northern Europe, a dark seed dropped by the high-precision pilot who then loops out and back to clear the impact zone.

Our truck bounced onto a metal ramp. All three of us lurched forward to steady the crate, nearly tipping it. Perez dropped his carbine. It rattled across the pickup's metal floor. Leaving the ramp, we bounced again. I thought Cairns was going to have a stroke.

He recovered by yelling at the tiny window behind the driver. "Hey! For Christ sake! Keep your goddam eyes on the road!"

At last we reached the hardstand where our plane was parked, a long barrel, highly polished, starting to roar somewhere behind its oval mouth, in the vicinity of its stubby, swept-back wings. Gingerly we unloaded the crate and turned it over to a crew-chief who had the flinty eyes that seemed to go along with the word *sergeant,* a man unflustered by the real thing.

Out on the runway, a plane was taking off, already rigged for its mission. Near us another plane taxied, waiting, inhaling with impatient snorts and flashing howls of airstream. Red Alert meant each pilot would simulate part of his target plan, fly out almost to the point of no return, then return to base. But at any moment it could become, as the colonels liked to say at staff meetings, "a real shootin match," a phrase they tossed around rather hopefully.

With relief I signed another piece of paper. An airman began to take apart the crate.

I was climbing into the pickup when I saw the pilot sprinting for his plane. I recognized the stride, and the build. He and I were neighbors in the village—a softspoken fellow about my age, from upstate Michigan. A white helmet covered his forehead, a gravity suit pressed at his waist and thighs. As he reached the plane he saw me, half raised one gloved hand, shouting something I could not understand. I shouted back but he didn't hear. Engine roar made speech almost impossible.

For a moment I was lost in an enormous silence, trying to hear something he had said just the previous weekend. I had run into him on one of my early morning strolls. He was wearing jeans then, an alpine sweater, standing outside the village church, breathing fog puffs and leaning in close to examine some masonry that went back to the Norman Conquest.

"Amazing, isn't it," he had said. "Nine hundred years of history right here in this old tower."

"Higher up," I had said, "some of the bricks are Roman. In those days they would just be lying around in the grass. The bricks, that is. The Romans were long gone."

"Amazing," he said again, shaking his head with a boyish grin. "The Romans. The Normans. Now us."

That was what struck me: Now us.

Under a high, dark fog, garish lamps lit the fuselage, the

pilot, the ladder. The roaring silence was like a huge pane of glass. Through it I watched him climb, watching through the kind of sound-proof glass that is both window and mirror. Somewhere in his cockpit there was a button he could push or a lever he could pull to release the canister. Until that moment I had not really believed he could do it, this fellow my age, this village neighbor with a sense of history. But I knew more about him now. I had carried the same little canister another mile along its path. And if this turned out to be the day he took it past the point of no return, would my name be stamped somewhere on it, next to his? I was not yet prepared to think about that.

I preferred to pull rank, to shout. I slammed the door and told the driver to step on it. He gave me a cautious look and said, "Relax, lootenant."

"Just get us the hell out of here!"

*

By the time we reached the shack we knew this was not going to turn into a real shootin match. At least not today. Not this morning. On his intercom the driver had picked up a raspy voice telling us the all-clear siren could be expected within an hour. Since our fellow couriers had not yet received this bit of news, Cairns and Perez and I could make the most of our return.

We came swaggering through the door, veterans who had been to the brink and back. I was squinting a little, the way patrol leaders are supposed to do, coming in out of heavy weather. I loosened my web belt and holster and canteen and dropped them heavily onto a metal chair.

Major Larkin stood up, still fully equipped. During alerts he never removed any of his battle gear. It was a point of honor. The helmet's steel lip seemed to rest on the rims of his glasses.

"How'd it go, Houston?"

"Not bad."

I unsnapped one side of my chinstrap and let it hang.

"They gave you a dummy, huh."

"Nope."

"A real one?" He said this with wide and wounded eyes.

"That's right."

Larkin took this personally. His feelings were hurt. In his two years as chief courier, he had never handled anything but a dummy.

"They didn't tell me we were going to be . . . uh . . ."

I pushed my helmet back and hardened my voice. "We happen to be in a Red Alert situation here, major."

"Well, look . . . uh, Houston . . . I mean, what was it like?"

I stood there trying to think of something clever or sarcastic that would devastate him. From the look in his eyes I knew he would take whatever I said. Once again I had him. But what was the point? Was Larkin my adversary? No. He was just a man, a very frightened man going for a pension, hoping the all-clear siren would keep blowing until he had his twenty years in.

Sarcasm failed me. What came to mind was another early morning, the first time my dad took me hunting, which was also the first time I watched an animal die at close range. I guess I was ten. It was a gray squirrel I had shot with my .22. It fell from a pine limb into the blanket of needles beneath the tree and twitched a few times before it expired. Watching the blood trickle I knew I was supposed to feel strong and proud. This was what we had been practicing for. This was why he had bought me the rifle. But I felt no pride. As he hunkered down to inspect the hole, I felt shame, and loneliness. He said it was not a bad shot at all and said we should keep the tail, which we did. It hung on the wall of my room for years.

I wish now I had described that incident to Larkin. It might have closed the space between us. But I couldn't. I couldn't speak. I walked to the coffee urn, poured a mugful, and returned to my folding chair in the far corner of the quonset hut. Unbuttoning my shirt to retrieve *The Telegraph* I spilled coffee across the front page. I was shaking all over, just from peeking through the window of war. I looked around, relieved to find myself suddenly alone. I looked at the stain and at the coffee jiggling, slopping at the rim. I tried to steady it. Finally I set it on the floor.

The Kung Fu Teacher With
Eyes Like G. Gordon Liddy

At the kung fu academy, where they have a summer introductory offer, my son has just finished his first month of lessons. I am here to see how he is doing. I step past a curtain of Chinese dragons that hangs in the doorway to the teacher's office. He is not Chinese, though there might be Apache in his background, or Basque. He is tall and lithe, with high cheekbones, black hair. His black eyes are so wide open and direct I have to attribute it to something, speed perhaps, or the concentration they say the martial arts require.

"I like what you told them," I say, "about not taking things personally."

He steps in very close to me and repeats what he just told his roomful of kids as they sparred around on the padded floor in their white jackets and new belts. "You can't over-react," he says. "Suppose some guy lands a little blow on your face . . ."

With a quick light jab he punches himself in the jaw.

"You don't want to drop into a crouch and get ready to kill."

He drops into just such a crouch. It is a move so sudden and threatening, I glance behind me to see who else has entered the office. But we are in here alone. As I turn back to the teacher he flicks out a fist I barely see, then the other fist. He reverses his stance, as if prepared to kick. His eyes now are more than alert. They blaze with deadly fire.

He straightens up, at ease again, and the fire subsides. "That is

77

when you have to cool it," he says. "This is a learning situation, right? The sparring and all. You are not out there to get even or anything."

I nod sagely. "You're out there to learn your moves."

"At some point, of course, you want the experience with contact. Because contact is what it's all about. If you only practice the moves and never feel the contact, you are living an illusion. All you have is form, right? Say you are out on the street, somebody starts something. You are only used to making the move but holding back on final contact. Some guy lands one on you, you could fold up right there . . ."

The fist snaps out again, like the head of a striking cobra, this time to within a millimeter of my chest. I see a little quiver in the knuckles before it snaps back and strikes again. Three strikes like that, snap, snap, snap, so fast the hand blurs, each one so close, the knuckles graze my shirt. In his eyes I see the sudden fire that looks and feels like rage. His moves seem to release it, while the rage gives each move its tight precision, its fierce restraint.

"I am not into violence," he says, as if answering a question I have almost put into words. "But there is no doubt that violence is where it's at. I mean, people are violent. And you can walk away from that fact or you can meet it head-on. You can allow the violence within yourself to be expressed. I refuse to retreat from that part of myself."

Now he is moving around the office, his voice rising, his panther muscles loose yet taut, ready to spring.

"You take movies nowadays. I don't think they should necessarily dwell on as much violence as they do. But when people sit through all these super-bloody movies we are getting, I think this is what they are looking for. It is like finally acknowledging something about yourself. I think you come out of that movie a more honest person. And maybe there is a connection here. I don't know. I have only been involved in one little incident that you couldn't even begin to call a fight. It wasn't a fight. It never went that far. Somebody got wise with me outside a theatre one night and I just made a couple of moves to let him know I wasn't kidding around . . ."

He is in front of me, crouching. Razor palms slice the air. The cobra-arm jabs. Then the powerful leg juts up and out. His foot is in the air between my shoulder and my face, as lethal as an ax and so close I can study the trimmed ivory nail on his big toe. Beyond the toe I see the taut leg and taut body in its sheath of eternal readiness, and then the black eyes again, watching me from the half-turned face with a degree of intensity I have seen once before, when I met G. Gordon Liddy at the annual convention of the American Booksellers Association in Los Angeles in 1979. He was there in suit and tie, a man who had devoted many years to patriotic assault, now signing copies of a new novel, after a short prison term for his part in the Watergate Hotel fiasco. Looking into the eyes of G. Gordon Liddy was like crash-landing at night, on the island of Java, and emerging hours later, after hacking your way through miles and miles of equatorial underbrush only to arrive at the base of a cliff where two cave openings look out upon the jungle, two impenetrable tubes of such unrelieved blackness they might be the entrances to ancient lava tubes that spiral inward, filled with frozen heat.

The kung fu teacher's rigid leg drops to the floor. His arms relax, and he falls back into the black padded chair next to his desk. His lips part in a broad and dazzling smile.

"I just caught the guy on the cheek with my foot, and it surprised the hell out of him, and I realized then how much power you can have, almost without even trying, because you see, I wasn't really ready to fight the guy. I was just sort of sending out this trial balloon."

The Lost Brother

This story has been on my mind for years, the story of a German drifter and his silent Swedish partner and the quiet beach they took me to, which seemed at the time to be the quietest in the world. It was a place where nothing moved, where water met the shore like a curving sheet of silver, cut to fit. The beach was made of round stones that clinked when you walked. For twenty-five years their sound has stayed with me, the dull clinking of porous stones beneath a pearl-gray sky. They had the same effect a wooden mallet can have as it strikes a wooden gong outside a buddhist temple, creating around it an enormous space, and you find yourself releasing into that space unremembered memories, feelings you did not know you had.

I was on an open ended trip, hitchiking south from Stockholm to Halsingborg, where I would eventually catch a ferry and cross to Denmark. Hitchikers were everywhere that summer, stacked up beyond the towns, strung along both sides of every junction. Rides were scarce, but it didn't matter much. The sun was warm, the skies were clear. I had just finished three years with the Air Force, in England, and had taken an overseas discharge. It was enough, being on the loose, with no orders to follow but my own.

I must have been standing in the same spot for two hours when a vehicle finally slowed down, a large vehicle, perhaps a moving van, though it bore no markings. I watched it roll for another thirty yards, saw the front wheels turn, as if the driver had changed his mind. The brake lamps flashed, and the great square-back rig stood vibrating in the golden morning light. After a moment the horn beeped. The passenger-side door flew open with a clang. A wild, leering, almost handsome face leaned out.

"Hey! What're you waiting for?"

I jogged down there, hoisting my back to the extended arm, which was lean and brown. He wore jeans and heavy boots, but no shirt.

"Don't use the bottom step," he said, laughing, "because it's gone."

I clambered up and in, just as the van's forward lurch slammed the door and propelled me past the wide front seat, which was the only seat. Two men and a young woman were pressed shoulder to shoulder, all of them shiny with sweat. Most of the van was empty. Its metal cavern seemed to collect and hold heat. Within fifteen seconds I too was sweating. I didn't mind. I set my pack against one wall and leaned back, glad to be rolling.

"Thanks for the lift," I said.

My shirtless host called over his shoulder, "You're American."

"That's right."

"You got any cigarettes?"

"I don't carry them. Sorry."

He gave me a mock-scowl, drooping his mouth like a circus clown and turned to the blond-haired fellow behind the wheel. "Hey Oly, we better kick this guy out. He don't have any cigarettes."

Oly wore a white undershirt, jeans, boots. He smiled,

eyes on the road. "Lucky for you," he said, in thickly accented English. "You already been smoking too much."

He aimed his bland eyes in my direction. "Where you going?"

"South."

He seemed to approve of this reply. "Goot," he said, with another smile.

The young woman between them was also blond, wearing a tank top, sipping from a beer bottle. She handed it to the shirtless one who now announced that his name was Rudy and the girl's was Ingrid, but Ingrid spoke no English so he would translate as necessary. He repeated all this in Swedish, then in German, watching her greedily, performing for her. She did not look at him. Tipping the bottle back for a long swallow, he deliberately spilled beer across her shoulder. He licked it off and pressed his lips to her ear, muttering in Swedish. With a sly glance toward me he muttered the English version. "You love Rudy, don't you."

From behind I saw her shoulders lift, which could have been a reaction to the beer his tongue had missed.

Rudy drank again and offered me a bottle. "We got plenty. Good Danish beer, better than anything you find in Sweden. But don't tell Oly you heard me say that."

I said anything wet would taste very good.

"First show me where you hide your cigarettes," he said. "Americans are always tall and they always have cigarettes. You want to do me a favor sometime, send me a carton from the states. Any brand."

He swung around to look at me, to share this little joke and to share a lecherous, man-to-man glance behind Ingrid's back. His hair was black. His face was triangular and as brown as the rest of him, which made his teeth doubly white when he grinned and laughed. I liked Rudy's laugh. It was soft and reckless. It drew me to him. For reasons I did not yet understand, we were drawn to each other. Nationality itself had a lot to do with this, the mystique of nationality, the fact that he was German and I was American and World War Two was still a recent memory.

In my eyes Rudy was exotic. Though I had been three years in Europe I had met few Germans, never sat in close quarters with a German who spoke English. During those same three years I had often seen the ruins of London buildings bombed by the Luftwaffe during the 1940s, roofless hulks around heaps of rubble, still waiting to be restored or demolished. It was impossible to look at that and not be reminded of the Luftwaffe and Gestapo movies I had grown up with. This was the summer of 1960. Fifteen years earlier Rudy and I would have been enemies. Now he was giving me a ride, and in this quick glance behind Ingrid's back he was giving me a naked look.

At close range I could see that, for all the laughter in his voice, there was none in his eyes. They were haunted and tortured eyes. For a moment they were searching mine, expecting something—if not cigarettes, then perhaps some other offering. It was just a flicker, before he handed me the beer and draped a possessive arm across her shoulder.

He had been drinking, he said proudly, since they left Stockholm. It was a way to relieve the tedium of this trip, which had been a weekly event for the past three or four years. "We also pick up people if we feel like it," he said. "Oly, he gets tired of my stories. So we met Ingrid last week in Halsingborg. She rode with us to Stockholm, on to Uppsala, back to Stockholm, and we all went dancing in a club I would like to show you sometime, a very dark and smokey club where jazz musicians play, sometimes American jazz musicians. Now she is riding home. But maybe not. Who knows? Maybe she cannot tear herself away from me. Maybe she will become a partner and ride with us forever."

Rudy flung his arms around as he talked, turning to me, bending to nuzzle Ingrid, who just sat there, lovely and suntanned and stoic, perhaps understanding him, perhaps not. Oly nodded from time to time. His easy grin rose and fell, though I was never sure what triggered it, a remark by Rudy, or an inner voice reminding him of some rich irony, perhaps the irony of his life. It was a very private and meditative grin.

Gradually I saw that I had been brought on board to witness Rudy's commentary. The Swedes were not giving him much satisfaction. He was a compulsive talker, who required an audience, and I had been chosen. This was fine with me. I was willing to listen, and he liked that. He needed that.

I soon learned that he and Oly were freelance haulers, moving furniture mostly, from Stockholm to the far south, or sometimes taking the coast road north, and back again to Stockholm, up and down the country, up and down. This van was their livelihood and often their portable motel. They carried food and bedding and extra clothes. They were beatniks who had never heard of Jack Kerouac. They were moving van gypsies, stopping here and there, whenever they had the urge, and today they planned to visit a beach that Rudy claimed was "a beach like no other you have ever seen!"

It meant a long detour, fifty kilometers west of the trunk route. But I had no fixed agenda, and by the time he brought this up I was into my third bottle, awash with fraternal goodwill.

He was into his fifth or sixth. "You must join us!" he cried, with a flourish that sent loose beer across the cab to splatter Oly's undershirt. "Forget your plans! Forget your cares! Forget your obligations! You cannot go anywhere else until you have seen this beach!"

His voice made it an invitation and a challenge and an arrogant boast. His melancholy eyes made it a plea I could not ignore. He wanted to show me something, and whatever this was, I wanted to see it.

*

Oly reached the clearing by early afternoon. We tumbled out of the overheated truck into an offshore breeze. I was near the cliff edge, to breathe a few lungfuls of sea air, when Rudy called out. "No! Don't look yet! Wait! Wait til we get to the bottom! From here you can see nothing! You have to feel it! You have to feel and look at the same time!"

We all pulled on shirts and sweaters and followed him down a steep path that dropped through scrub brush toward the shoreline. He had an arm around Ingrid, dragging her along, shouting as he jostled her on and off the trail. She encouraged this, laughing with him, pushing back at him each time he pushed, ignited now, and playful. But as we neared the bottom, the silliness faded, and with it all their shouting and banter. Something in the atmosphere said, *Hush*. There was no other sound, no surf breaking, no wind, no seabirds. The sky was a roof of luminous gray, beneath which I felt suddenly small. It lent a sheen to the endless stretch of still water. Cliffs rose, back from the water, and between the cliffs and the sea lay a field of pinkish-gray stones, rolled smooth by the tides. For acres they spread among ragged spires that had once been connected to the line of cliffs.

Rudy had stopped to contemplate the scene, his trucker's boots planted. His mouth still smirked, after a last reach for Ingrid's buttocks. But his eyes had changed. He looked at me, to gauge my reaction, and I thought I saw reverence there. His whole manner had changed. With a long, careful stride he stepped out across the beach, devoutly picking his way, the sober pilgrim. Behind him we fell into single file, Oly, then me, then Ingrid. No one spoke. With each step, stones touched. Their clinking cut a path of sound through the silence.

Halfway across the beach he stopped again, pointing up toward a patch of moss on a sloping ledge. In that silvery light, every touch of color shimmered with its own aura—Ingrid's bronze face, Oly's blond hair, his pale Nordic eyes, Rudy's blue workshirt. High above us this mossy patch was a vibrant green cushion among the jagged rocks.

Rudy said, "Let's climb up there."

Oly shook his head, with a little shrug, as if he knew this was coming or had done it before and did not need to do it again. "Too much," he said.

Ingrid had fallen far behind, poking around at the water's edge, as if searching for something she had dropped. Rudy was already climbing, shouting in Swedish. Oly laughed. With hands on hips he watched his goat-partner scramble upward. Winking at me he turned and moved away toward the water.

I followed Rudy. It was a steep climb, but not difficult. In five minutes we were sitting on the green moss, surveying the world. Far below we saw Ingrid and Oly, very small, close together where the water touched the stones. We watched them walk arm in arm away from the water.

"Look at that," Rudy said. "Disgusting, eh? The way women treat you?"

"I don't know what she sees in Oly," I said, trying to keep it light. "He's just another pretty face."

This amused him. If he was feeling a pang of loss, it seemed to pass as soon as they disappeared behind a rocky overhang. Out of sight, out of mind. He leaned back on his

elbows, drinking in the view, which was now unob-
structed, unpeopled. From this high vantage point the
width of the sea and sky had tripled. And something about
our altitude made the quiet more profound. I felt I could
hear the tiny crackle of my own nerve-ends straining to listen. In such a place, any speech would be superfluous.
And yet, after a while, you felt compelled to speak, if only
to test the depth of the silence. That, at any rate, is what I
heard in Rudy's voice, which was much subdued when he
spoke again.

Softly he said, "I come here a lot. It makes me feel
peaceful. You know what I mean? It is the best place I
found in Sweden. It is the only place I ever found that can
make me feel this way."

His voice was dry, thick with emotion, and he was smiling slightly, measuring me through half closed eyes. With a
sly and amiable sideways glance he said, "Sometimes I
come down here, I don't talk at all. I sit, and I listen.
But . . . maybe it is because you are American, and that
starts me thinking . . . You mind if I tell you something?"

He wasn't looking at me then. He was studying the sky,
and I knew he was about to tell me the story of his life.

"Before I found this beach I used to think about going
back to Germany. A few times I almost did. I got tired of
Sweden. That's when I thought about going back. But I
never could. I knew it would be worse for me there than
here. I think about what Germany did in the war, and I
cannot go back. That was why I got my Swedish citizen-
ship. The funny thing is, I feel bad about *not* going back,
about running away. It is my country. I mean, it was. I
used to think I hated Germany. Now I am not so sure. I
don't know what I think. I just know I can't go back.
When I was fifteen they made me join the army. Me and
my brother. You ever hear about Hitler Youth? We were in

it. I was fifteen. He was sixteen. This was right at the end of the war, nobody left to put into the army but kids. They sent us to the Russian front . . ."

He stopped and leaned back against the slope of moss, struggling with something. I did not know what to say. I only knew I was there to witness whatever he needed to reveal. I waited a couple of minutes and decided to tell him I too had spent some time in the military, had just been released from duty, and this had left me with many questions about America I had not yet answered. With no war on, my experience had not come close to his, I said, but perhaps it gave me some feeling for what he was talking about. I told him I too had thought about not returning home.

As I said this, it occurred to me that I should explain what I meant. But from the way he continued to watch the sky I wasn't sure he had been listening.

I waited, and in the silence a memory began to form. I didn't know why. It was a forgotten scene I had been carrying around for over a year, a crash-landing right after take-off, and the death of a pilot at age twenty-three. I knew him slightly, a hotshot, a dreamer. His engine had flamed out before he had enough altitude to eject. He tried to bring the plane down in a field beyond the runway, and the impact had killed him. He was a warrior, in a way, a fighter-bomber pilot, but this had been a routine training mission which actually made it worse, to see a fellow of that age, my age, taken out by mere equipment failure. It was the kind of loss you cannot blame any one person for so you end up blaming everyone, the maintenance crew, the Wing Commander, the defense contractor, the Pentagon, governments that keep us always on the brink . . .

"When the Russians finally won," he said, "I ran away and burned my uniforms."

Rudy's words cut through my revery. In the still air they cut a path, like the beach stones touching.

"I went over with them and worked polishing boots, doing little odd jobs for the officers. Later, when I was still fifteen, I worked for the Americans. I liked them better. They gave me cigarettes. They got them free and gave them away all the time. They gave me lots of things because I worked good for them, for almost a year. And that was the first time I had enough to eat since before the war, the time I worked for the American soldiers. In the army I never had enough. At home, during the war, never."

The moist gratitude now filling his eyes was aimed at me. His face opened up in a playful grin. "Hey. You *sure* you don't have a cigarette? That's what I need right now, more than anything."

I made a show of patting all my pockets and feigned apology for running out. He shrugged elaborately, feigning forgiveness, then looked away again, as if something offshore caught his eye.

"When I was sixteen I had to get out of Germany. I mean, I wanted to. There was nothing for me there. All my relatives had been killed. Everyone. No family. I sailed a boat with another fellow over here to Sweden, and the Swedes stopped us and wanted to know who we were. When we said Germans, they wouldn't let us in. They made us sail back. A month later we tried again, in a different boat. This time we said we were Russians. I had learned some Russian, you see, and so they let us in. Crazy, eh? So I been in Sweden ever since. And after a while I started to read newspapers in Swedish, later some books. I learned what Germany did in the war, and what I fought for, and what my brother died for. I watched him die, you know, shot in the head when he was sixteen. By a

Russian soldier. I have a picture of my brother with his helmet split open. In here I have a picture . . ."

He pointed to his forehead.

"For years I dreamed about it, and it would wake me up night after night. I do not dream so much any more. But it is always there."

Rudy's voice had opened me. While he saw his brother, I was seeing another face and another helmet—the pilot again, in the seconds before they had him out of there and into an ambulance. As Information Officer it was my job to be at any accident site ahead of the local reporters. This time I happened to reach the end of the runway just as the fire team tore back his canopy. He was sitting up straight, a pilot-mannequin. The eyes were open, the mouth seemed about to speak. Framed by the white helmet, the face still had color, a flawless duplicate of a living face.

It was my first look into the mirror of untimely death. For weeks afterward I was angry. But I had not wept. A year later it came welling up, as the story of Rudy's brother unlocked grief for the young pilot, and then revealed an older, deeper grief which took me completely by surprise.

Rudy was blinking back the moisture now, blinking hard. "Sometimes I start feeling sorry for myself," he said. "You ever do that? I start thinking how my brother's life was cut short, so he never had a chance. And me, after I was twelve, I never went back to school. So now I am nothing. A truck driver. A bum. But still, I am alive. And I think about my brother who never even had a chance to do . . . this."

He was weeping openly, silently. I was weeping with him, for the older brother he had lost, and for the lives they could have led together, and now for someone I had lost—

not the pilot, but a brother who had never been born, a brother who had been inhabiting the same invisible realm of unexamined memories. That's all he was, a memory that came floating to the surface unannounced, with no dimension, no specific features, nothing else to go on. I had never thought about him, nor had anyone in my family ever talked about him much. I had only heard him mentioned once or twice, and then obliquely. This almost-brother was stillborn when I was two, an event so surrounded with silence it had become non-memory. Sitting there above the quiet beach, mourning for companionships that might have been, I began to see for the first time how the non-existence of this unborn brother has worked on me.

We sat staring out to sea until a fishing boat appeared, inside the horizon, as gently as a handkerchief offered up to dry our eyes. It was a fisherman rowing toward the beach—a sign of life, of life continuing, of other humans going about their daily tasks. For a long time we watched and did not speak. Eventually the sound of oars reached us, like a faraway dripping—chick, chick—as they touched the water. We watched and listened until he stepped out of the boat and pulled it onto the stones, scraping, clinking. He wore a cap and a heavy sweater and moved like an older man. When he had pulled the boat clear he shambled away. The sound under his shoes rose up to us, as if amplified. The clink of other footsteps seemed to follow him, and soon we saw Oly and Ingrid re-appear, arms around waists, drawing from Rudy his sardonic laugh.

"You see the kind of partner I have? He is so foolish he thinks this is a beach you bring girls to. I tried it once. That was plenty. It is how I found this place. I picked up a girl in one of these towns and Oly had another one and he wanted the van. There is plenty of room in the van for four people, but Oly is that way. He wants room. I had to let him have the whole van because he owned more of it than me then. So I was looking for another place and we came down here. After dark it is a hell of a place to take a girl, and I don't just mean the rocks. But that is how I found it. Maybe four years ago. After I was in this damn country ten years. Since then I stop here almost every trip. It makes me feel good. I don't forget, you see. I never forget anything. But I feel peaceful here. It lets things out. I like to bring my friends here so they can feel it too."

His dark eyes looked to be on the edge of mischief, as if he were going to ask one more time for the mythical cigarette. But he didn't. He jumped to his feet and began the descent, from boulder to boulder, with his long careful stride.

By the time we had crossed the beach and climbed the scrubby path that led us to the clearing, Oly and Ingrid were already inside. The engine was chattering. With an impatient clang, Rudy hurled open the door, shouting in three languages, digging around underneath the seat, throwing all his empties out into the gravel. He plopped down next to ingrid and squeezed her.

"Hey. You seen my whiskey?"

She reached behind the seat and produced a half-empty pint. He said, "You love Rudy, don't you." As he tried to kiss her, she opened the bottle and held it to his lips. He drank like a baby, then drew away from her and began to sing a German song. He was drunk again and wild again and amorous again, performing again, all the way to Halsingborg, where there was a warehouseman to be met late that day, a roomful of furniture to be looked at, in advance of loading up the next morning.

It was still light when they dropped me at the wharf, in time to catch the last ferry, for the short trip across the straits to Copenhagen. We all shook hands and said we knew we would meet again. Next time, Rudy said, we would plan to start earlier and travel farther and drink more. Then I was shouldering my pack and he was slamming the door, with one last wave, his whole arm and chest out the window, his manic leer.

As the van pulled away, something came clear to me. I saw how I had for years been searching the faces of men around my age, or a few years younger or a few years older, collecting brothers, looking for the brother I almost had. It occurred to me that his non-life, and the wispy legend of his stillborn near-arrival, had created in me a vacant place, a yearning for a certain kind of comradeship, along with the fear that it would always elude me.

I stood there wishing I had thought of this five minutes sooner, so I could have found a way to express it to Rudy. But the van was gone. They were halfway across town, heading for the warehouse, and tomorrow on to Stockholm, while I had a ferry to catch, moving south and west, toward England, and eventually home.

Part Two:
HEROES AND
ANCESTORS

The Dangerous Uncle

If you would be unloved and forgotten,
be reasonable.
> from *God Bless You, Mr. Rosewater* (1965)
> by Kurt Vonnegut, Jr.

He was the renegade, the one who could not be tamed or domesticated, the wild card in the family. Was he my favorite uncle? No. But he was by far the most attractive, a man who could not hold his liquor or his money or any of the numerous women who passed through his life. Among my father's four brothers he was the closest in age, so they had grown up together in east Texas, Dudley and Anderson, companions and cohorts, two years apart. I have seen my father rigid with fury at something this brother had recently done to him. I have also watched him laugh as he recounted a boyhood stunt that foreshadowed the kind of life Anderson would lead. I mention this because my father was not what I would call an outgoing or expansive man. He was not given to shows of pleasure, yet Anderson could make him laugh aloud.

"I remember a day we were down along the creek," he told me once, "and back in that part of Texas the creek was the only place where you could cool off in the summer. I guess I was around twelve and Andy was around fourteen. He had this trick he liked to do, just to show off. He used to do it at school until the teachers made him quit. He was always real limber, you see. He had a way of putting one foot up behind his head, like a Hindu, and he was mighty proud of himself whenever he got his foot up there, since he was the only one in our family who could do that.

"Well sir, on this particular day, just about the time we had our shirts pulled off, but still had our trousers on, a couple of girls came walking along the creek trail. Anderson decided he would show them something they would never forget, and he commenced to shove his whole foot and ankle up behind his head. The girls saw that and they got to giggling and ran on down the creek. Anderson got to laughing so hard he fell over. He'd been standing on one leg, ya see, like a stork. For a while he was laying there in the dirt by the creek laughing til the tears ran down his face. Then he quit laughing and looked up at me with this funny look, and he said, Hey Dudley, come over here and give me a hand, will ya, while I get my foot down.

"I went over there and pushed and pulled a while, with him telling me what to do and where to grab hold. But it turned out there wasn't much either one of us could do because his foot was just plain stuck. He had shoved it over too far and got his neck turned some kind of way, and I had to leave him there and run back home to get my dad and our oldest brother, who was already grown, and stronger than anybody else too, because he did pushups and lifted weights, and bring them down there. It was a mile to the house and a mile back. Before we got near where he was we could hear Anderson yelling. His leg had cramped up. He thought he was going to die alone by the creek bank with one foot locked behind his head."

The way dad told it, that was the prelude to Anderson's entire career—the family clown and a born nuisance, always leaving a mess behind that someone else had to come along and clean up. It was also the longest story I can remember hearing him tell. He was not a talkative man, yet he would talk about Anderson. I think he had to, there was so much to get off his chest. Anderson called things out of him no one else could call out. My dad was not given to shows of anger. Yet this brother could make him curse and slam a fist into the side of the house. He was not a violent man, but one day Anderson made him angry enough to kill.

This happened after we moved south into Santa Clara Valley, where dad had picked up a few acres with a house and outbuildings. During our years in San Francisco, one of his dreams had been to get out of the city and back to the land. In the late 1940s, the valley had not yet begun to bulge and multiply and become the high-tech headquarters it is today. It was still one huge orchard. Out near the western foothills we had a small piece of it, with some fruit trees, a barn, a greenhouse.

Not long after we made this move, Anderson started showing up three or four times a year. He liked it there, since he shared dad's taste for the rural life. They shared a few other things too, but in certain crucial ways these two brothers were like day and night. Dad was a quiet and inward man. Anderson was a compulsive talker. Dad was anchored. Anderson was not. He had gone through five wives and countless jobs, and now he was drifting back and forth between Texas and California. Dad would allow him to stay, sometimes for months, because they had grown up together, and because he was the brother with nowhere else to go, and because Anderson would talk him into it, and because Anderson, when sober, was a man of many talents. Perhaps too many.

He was a carpenter. He was a gardener. He was a mechanic. He could sink postholes and erect a fence that ran straight and true. One summer I watched him take over a picking crew, become foreman for a rancher we knew, and get twenty acres of apricots gathered in record time. For a number of years before the war, Anderson made a good living as a hairdresser in Los Angeles. He changed his name to *Andre*, and he took advantage of the fact that in their boyhood section of Texas the nearest town of any size had been Paris. He became "An-dray from Par-ee." With his wavy hair and his rascal's grin and his gift of gab, it worked. He made and spent a lot of money.

When World War Two came along he joined the army and travelled the Pacific with a construction battalion, Hawaii, New Guinea, the Aleutians. The heavy drinking started then and led to a stomach ulcer that finally put him in an army hospital. No one could say it was the army or the war that disabled him, but he left the service with a disability pension and a chronic condition that had him moving in and out of V.A. hospitals for years. Mostly out. He wouldn't sit still for treatment. He would check himself in on a Monday. By Tuesday night he would be sneaking out the side door, carrying his shoes.

If medicine was prescribed, he wouldn't take it. If advice was given—such as Stop drinking—he would listen a while, then forget. Twice he joined A.A., and twice he backslid. By the time we were installed in Santa Clara Valley he was living on his pension checks, which he tended to blow as soon as one arrived in the mail. His monthly binge could end with a phone call from a bar in Salinas. Or it could be a call from an all-night service station in Reno, someone saying, "Mr. Houston? We got a fella here out of gas and out of money sittin in a vegetable truck that isn't his and he can't remember where he got it, who says you're his brother and not to call the police til we call you first . . ."

Dad would slam the phone down and say that as of to-day Andy would have to take care of himself because this was absolutely the last time he was going to bail him out of anything!

The next day they would both appear in the driveway side by side in our pickup, my dad stoic, the survivor who had come west during the 1930s with seven dollars in his pocket and now had seven acres with a house in the coun-try, and Anderson, disheveled, hangdog, the prodigal brother with nowhere to lay his head.

We would soon learn he had promised dad something. We would usually learn it from Anderson himself, as we sat around the supper table. And I should point out that in those days I did not yet know the broken pattern of his life. I only heard his Southern Comfort voice, saw the crafty eyes of the garrulous uncle, the colorful uncle, the uncle you hoped would stay for a while.

"Some people are slow learners," he would say, as he dove into his first solid meal in a week, talking between mouthfuls of biscuits and gravy, pork chops, blackeyed peas. "And you people are looking at the slowest learner of all time. But I'll tell you right now, ol Andy has learned his lesson at last. I have taken my final drink. I swear it. Dudley here is my witness. You are all my witnesses. If it wasn't for Dudley, I would be a goner. I would be breathing my final breath in the darkest gutter of the skid rows of Los Angeles, and nobody knows that better than I do. I tell ya . . ."

Now tears would be glinting in his red-rimmed eyes, as he paid tribute to all the many ways my father had saved him from himself. "I tell ya, I am going to make it up to you, Dudley. I am going to make it up starting tomorrow. Starting tonight! We've got a couple of hours of daylight left. Soon as we finish supper I am going to go out there and get started on that chicken house roof. Yes sir. I am gonna get a new roof on your chicken house, so them white leghorns will sleep cozy. Then I'm gonna run that fence down along to the end of the property line like I started to do last spring. And listen. Let me tell all of you right now, help me stay away from the mailbox. I mean it! I don't want to *see* that pension check. I don't even want to see a calendar. That way I'll lose track of time and won't know which day of the month it is and won't even know when to look for that check, because that check belongs to *Dudley*! You all hear me now? You are talking to a man who is making a fresh start!"

I should also point out that dad's vision of how things could look around the place ran far ahead of his available time. There was always brush to be cleared or the barn to be patched, a chimney to rebuild, a bedroom to add on, an acre of trees to prune. He was working fulltime as a painting contractor, and the weekends were never long enough. My mother meanwhile had her hands full managing the house, tending her flowers outside the house, keeping me and my sister in school clothes, and giving any spare hours to the vegetables. In this little world Anderson's skills were much appreciated, particularly when it came to the chickens, which played a key role in my father's dream. A well managed chicken pen would provide the eggs and the meat to complement the tomatoes and the corn and the greens that would emerge from the year-round garden. Building up his flock little by little, he had accumulated thirty white leghorns and a few Rhode Island Reds. He had recently widened the pen with new fencing. Anderson must have known, consciously or unconsciously, that the henhouse roof was right at the top of dad's long list of chores, and the very offer that would soften his heart.

So once again he stayed, and two months went by without incident. Fresh loam soon darkened all the flower beds. New gravel appeared in the driveway. Borders of brick and river-stones had encircled the fruit trees nearest the house. At night, around the table we would listen to him talk, and this in itself was worth a lot. Dad never talked much at the table. He ate in silence, thinking about what had to be done tomorrow.

Two months like this, then one night the supper table was quiet again. My father, home late and coming in from the garage just as the food was set out, looked around the kitchen and said, "Andy lost his appetite?"

My mother said, "I thought maybe he was with you today."

"Why would he be with me?"

"I sure haven't seen him around here."

He thought about this and started to eat. After a while he said, "What day is it?"

"Thursday."

"What day of the month?"

"The second."

He thought again and ate some more. "I suppose if you brought in the mail yesterday there is no way he could have got his hands on that pension check."

"I thought you brought the mail in yesterday," my mother said.

"How could I bring in the mail when I wasn't here."

"I told you I had to go shopping."

"You don't have to go shopping right when the mailman is coming up the road."

"I can't spend my whole life walking back and forth to the mailbox, Dudley."

This came out sharp. When he didn't respond, she softened. "One time that check didn't get here until the third or the fourth. The way he keeps changing addresses, it's a wonder it ever gets here at all."

"He wouldn't take off by himself if he didn't have any money."

"Did you look in your clothes closet?"

"I'd better do that," he said, pushing his chair back.

If anything was missing, a jacket, or one of dad's favorite shirts, it meant Anderson was gone and did not plan to return for quite some time. But nothing was missing, which meant the phone could ring at any moment. Dad sat down at the table again and pursed his lips and narrowed his eyes and looked out into the dusk, waiting for that call, already bracing for it.

For three days he waited, then he began to worry that something might have happened, something worse than drunkeness. On the night of the third day he drove around to the nearest saloons. No one had seen Andy.

The next afternoon I was out in front of the house trying to straighten the handlebars on my one-speed when he reappeared, carrying what looked like a square cage. He wasn't staggering. He was very erect, walking with his shoulders back, planting his feet like a mountaineer starting a long climb, though there was no mountain. The road was flat.

He called out, "Jimmy! How you doin, son?"

"I'm doin fine, uncle Anderson. How you doin?"

"I got somethin for ya," he said.

As he approached, I looked again at the cage, trying to see through its close wire mesh. There was something alive inside, eager to get out. But that was not what he meant. From his scuffed-up leather jacket he withdrew a photograph and handed it to me with a wink. It was a folded and rumpled but still glossy eight-by-ten of a young woman in a skimpy white swimsuit, early Jayne Mansfield perhaps, or someone of her proportions. I don't have a clear memory of the face. I was fourteen, and I was transfixed by the cleavage. I glanced at Anderson and saw him watching my hunger, the depraved uncle, the outlaw uncle, the uncle you wished would take you somewhere.

He winked again. "I got somethin for your daddy too," he said, lifting the lid of the cage an inch to reveal a beak, a glittering eye. Half a head forced its way out, black and fierce. Anderson pushed the lid shut.

"Your daddy is big on hens, but he is short on roosters. This is a little rooster I picked up over in San Jose. Fella I ran into raises em to fight. So they got plenty of spunk. This little black one here is the spunkiest chicken I have ever seen. It is just what your daddy needs to pep up his flock. You know what I mean? Cross breeding is what I'm talking about. Hybrid vigor."

Though I knew next to nothing about raising chickens, even less about fighting cocks, I knew this sounded like a dangerous idea. I also knew better than to stand in his way. There was whiskey on his breath, and smoke in his clothes, and in his eyes a glint just like that rooster's, somewhere between mischief and madness. Once before, when he was this far along, he had challenged me to a fight. With clenched fists swirling he had demanded that I punch him as hard as I could, to try for the face. If I was afraid to punch my own uncle in the face, he had cried, I was a yellow bellied coward and no nephew of his. Today he was on a kind of automatic pilot, he was walking and he was talking, but he was hearing no one, seeing nothing but some crazed vision of how this bird was going to transform his brother's flock—which of course it did.

Holding to his own straight and narrow course he

moved past the house, past the barn, around a corner of the pen. Once inside the gate, he set the cage down on its side and unlatched the lid.

The cock rushed out, with an impatient lift of sleek black wings, so black, in late sun, the close-trimmed feathers had a purple tinge. As if surprised to find no adversary there, it stopped in the middle of the yard, muscular and nervous, its head twitching, its tense legs ready to spring.

Anderson had probably picked up that bird right after a fight. Spurs were still tied to its heels, little knives that looked dark with what might have been blood, though I wasn't sure. He only stood still a few seconds. These cocks that have been trained to kill, they must feed on fear. It must bring out the worst in them. The leghorns had scurried for the fence, clucking and bunching. This black rooster went for the other males first, then started after the hens, ripping and slashing, jabbing at eyes, sometimes lifting off the ground to drive spurs into a defenseless breast or wing or rump.

I remember Anderson poised in the half-open gateway, for a long moment of stupefied horror, while a few birds made their escape between his legs. He began to kick at them, warning, "Look out now! Look out!" Then he was a barnyard dancer, waving his arms at the flurry, shouting, "Hyeah! Hyeah!" Wary of the rapier beak, he made some half-hearted lunges. Finally he yelled at me to go inside and get my .22.

Loading it took a while. The rifle stood behind my desk. The shells were in another room, one dad kept locked. By the time I came bounding through the back door, his pickup had pulled into the driveway. I watched him climb out and walk to the fence and gaze at what he knew was his brother's handiwork. Some birds had fluttered out the gate or into the safety of the henhouse. At least half were dead or badly wounded, flopping around with broken wings, broken backs, fluid running from a torn eye. It was a battlefield of feathers and carcasses, with one bird still on two feet, the spent but victorious killer cock, his black coat gleaming with blood.

For a silent minute dad surveyed this carnage. His teeth pressed together until the jaw muscles stood out like flat rocks inside his cheeks. Then he turned toward Anderson, sitting on the woodpile about twenty feet away with his face in his hands. Dad walked over to the chopping block, freed the hand axe and stood there until Anderson raised his head. Seeing the axe, he swallowed what he probably figured was going to be his final swallow.

Dad turned away and walked to the chicken pen and kicked open the gate and kicked leghorn carcasses out of the way. When he had the battle-weary rooster cornered, he grabbed it behind the neck in a grip so sudden and tight, the bird looked paralyzed. Squeezing it at arms length, he brought it back to the block. This seemed to revive the bird, whose squirming life-fear, in turn, revived Anderson. Cold sober now, his face filled with pleading, he looked up and said, "Don't do it, Dudley."

The hand axe rose, and Anderson said it again. "Please don't do it. That rooster cost me fifty dollars."

"FIFTY DOLLARS!" my father shouted. "That's damn near half your pension check!"

"That's what I'm trying to tell you."

The axe fell with such force, the blade sank two inches into the wood, while the black head went one way, and the rest of the bird went the other. They watched it run in circles, with blood spurting from the open neck, until the life was spent and it fell over into the dirt.

Quietly my father said, "I want you to go get that bird and pluck it."

Tears were streaming down Anderson's face, tears of relief that he himself was still alive. He said, "Pluck it?"

"I want you to pull out every last feather, and that in-
cludes the real small ones underneath the wings and inside
the legs."

"What for?"

"We're gonna eat that bird for dinner tonight. If it cost
fifty dollars, we might as well get some use out of it."

"I tried to bargain that fella down, Dudley. I swear I did.
But he just wouldn't listen. Fifty was his bottom offer."

Disgusted, my father stepped back into the pen, where he
began to clean up the mess, salvage what he could. He sent
me out to round up the strays. Anderson went to work on
the rooster. About an hour later he presented it to my
mother, who had come home from an afternoon's shopping
to find her dinner menu slightly revised. She had cooked a
lot of chickens, but never a fighting cock. She decided to
boil it, and she let it boil for a long time, hoping for some
kind of stew.

Late that night, when we sat down to supper, we discovered that boiling only made it tougher. In death as in life
that bird was solid muscle. Though narrow strips of flesh
could eventually be torn from the bone, they were unchew-
able. Several minutes of silent struggle passed before anyone dared to mention this.

With a hopeful grin Anderson said, "It's not that bad."

"I suppose I could have tried roasting it," my mother said.

"It's not that bad at all," Anderson went on, "consider-
ing the life this bird has led."

He winked at me and then at my sister, and we would
have laughed, were it not for the cloud hanging over the table, which was the great cloud of my father's disappointment in the brother who had gone too far. Anderson knew
this, even as he tried one more time to get a rise out of him.

"Fact a the matter is, what we're lookin at here is a fifty dollar dinner. Now I know you aint never had a dinner that was that expensive, Dudley. I'd say we're eatin mighty high on the hog tonight!"

Dad nodded. "I guess you're right, Andy. We'd have to drive clear to San Francisco to get a dinner that cost this much."

Anderson's laugh burst out, raucous and full of phlegm. He pounded on the table. "You kids hear what your daddy just said? We'd have to drive clear to San Francisco!"

His laugh filled the kitchen and went on for a long time, but all it drew from dad was a thin smile, a painfully courteous smile for the brother who had finally pushed him past his limit.

Years later we would all be able to laugh about that day, dad too, the way he laughed about the time Andy's foot got stuck behind his neck. I see now that Anderson had always been the one to do this for him, in a way no one else could—rile him, stir him, tickle his funnybone. But this time forgiveness was still a long way off. And it turned out to be the last night Anderson sat at our table.

As time went by, news would trickle our way, from other relatives who had taken him in, or invented reasons not to. For a while, as I heard the stories others had to tell, I thought dad had been too gullible, the way he had let Andy talk him into things year after year, then steal his clothes and his time and his trust. It's clear to me now that dad loved him more and had put up with his antics longer than anyone else had been able to.

I don't know what passed between them, in private, before he left, but he was gone the next morning, heading back to Texas, the dark uncle, the dangerous uncle, the uncle you never forget.

The New-Age Barber

He wears an aloha shirt, running shoes, and his blue eyes are full of amusement. Around my chin he tucks a white towel and tilts me back until my neck touches the cool and curving edge of his haircare sink.

"Just relax," he says, with his fingertips lightly cupping my ears. "This is something new. I don't think I've used it on you before, a shampoo especially for men. Takes care of certain oils and toxins."

"Men need a different shampoo from women?" I say.

"You know it. Things get produced by testosterone. Dandruff can also be a factor."

"You think testosterone and dandruff are related?"

"Stress is a factor too. It's all related. Hey, did you check out my new neon sign?"

"It's nice," I say, "very 80s."

"It's the coming thing. Neon is everywhere. Friends of mine, they have it in the bathroom, like somebody drew a stripe of purple light above the tub. A square purple halo."

"I hear neon doesn't cost as much to run."

"So they say. I haven't seen a bill yet. But yeah, it is supposed to cost a whole lot less. I don't know what to tell you about the radiation factor, whether or not you get zapped having it on all the time or what. Let's step into the other room now and get to work. Nobody can tell me

your *hair has stopped growing. How long has it been since you were in here anyway?"*

"A couple of months."

"That's about as far as I would push it. Six or seven weeks would be better. In your case. Now tell me what you're in the mood for. Punk? Rad? James Dean? Elvis? Flat top?"

"Don't laugh when you say flat top. They're coming back."

"Tell me about it. You see em everywhere."

"I used to have one."

"In the service?"

"In highschool. That was actually what started me going to a barbershop."

"You wanted the professional touch, right?"

"For years my dad cut my hair. Sometimes my uncle would, if he was around. They were both good. But my uncle was the champ. For a while he made a living at it, though he never considered himself a barber. He was a hairdresser. Or a hair designer."

"Hey, look at me. Am I a barber? I am a hair design technician. A grooming consultant. An appearance facilitator. I am just thinning back here, by the way, layering as I go. Basically what I did last time."

"I trust you. I'm not even watching."

"Maybe I will give myself a promotion to Skull Engineer and Master Stylist. My motto will be 'Everything above the neck.'"

"You would have liked my uncle."

"Why didn't you let him *do your flat top?"*

"He knew how. But he wouldn't. Maybe he thought it was beneath him."

"He wouldn't think that way now. There are guys downtown, barbers of what you might call the classic school, sitting in their shops since the 60s, paying rent and wondering what happened. They spend half the day alone worrying about their overhead and waiting to retire, and all of a sudden the great wheel turns and they are working again. They know how to do something the kids want. Flat tops are back in,

and these guys who learned how to do it on some destroyer out in the middle of the Pacific, they are cleaning up. You can see them in there buzzing away."

"How about you? If I wanted a flat top, could you handle it?"

"Not like the guys downtown. What they do in ten minutes, brrrrr-rrrrrp, brrrrrrrrp, brrrrrrrrp, with the electric clippers, would take me forty-five. I worry about every hair."

"I thought you just said you were a master stylist."

"Did I say I couldn't do one? Of course I can do one. I just have to get it, you know, really flat. But hey, you want a flat top, a butch, a G.I. high and dry? You want a double mohawk? You want dread locks? I am ready. I am a survivor, right? And the key to survival is versatility. That is what broke the hearts of the older generation, those guys downtown who only learned how to do three or four things, and when those three or four things went out of style, where were they? Reading back issues of THE POLICE GAZETTE. At least if my shop is empty, I have better magazines to look at. INTERVIEW. SPIN. VOGUE. ROLLING STONE. VANITY FAIR. But my shop is never empty, because I can do whatever is required. Now tell me something. Am I taking too much off the sides?"

"You're doing fine, just fine."

"Where was your uncle located?"

"Los Angeles, when he was in the business, said he used to work on film celebrities."

"Did he ever say who?"

"He kept that part vague."

"Yul Brynner? Eric Von Stroheim?"

"Something along those lines."

"They were both bald, of course."

"My uncle could have talked either one of them into a haircut. He was a born talker."

"That's probably why he cut hair."

"You could be right. My dad was almost as good with the scissors. But he never cared much for talking."

"Let me tell you, barbers are like bartenders. You have to like to talk to people. You ever had a silent haircut?"

"Not since I left home."

"Silence makes people nervous. They think something has gone wrong. They think some kind of judgment is being made about the places where the hair might be getting thin, or the condition of the skin or the knobs on the back of the skull. There is a kind of intimacy about this work that can make people very anxious. It's why dentists talk the way they do. By that I don't mean the amount of talking, but the times they choose to ask you a leading question, which is almost always the wrong time, when your mouth is so full of stuff you can hardly breathe. A tube is hanging off your lip, and the dentist is in there with his little flashlight and his pick, digging around, and right then is when he says something like, "Too bad about the playoffs." To which you can only grunt like a man coming down with lockjaw—unnnh awnnnhh innnnnhh. But what's going on is, you two are in this amazingly intimate relationship. How many people really know what is happening on the back side of your teeth, where things are crumbling and chipping off in the dark? Only your dentist. You are vulnerable, and he feels this crazy responsibility for putting you at ease by asking you about the playoffs. And the same thing is going on here in the grooming salon, where some guy like me is getting closer to your scalp and to the follicles on top of your head than anybody else on earth really cares to get. In this situation a little chitchat can ease the uncertainty factor. I know things about the top of your head you yourself will never know, because you can never see it from my perspective, unless I came in for a close-up shot with a wide-angle Polaroid, which would probably be more trouble than it's worth. Now tell me where you want the part. Right side. Or left."

"You always ask me where I want the part."

"That's because you always know the correct answer."

"Left."

"Of course. I can see it now. The hair naturally falls that way. The hair remembers. Only the hair technician forgets."

"You're forgiven."

"Don't move. I am just going to bring the edger in close to your ear one more time for some very fine tuning. When you walk out of here you're going to look so good, you might stop traffic. Be sure to check both ways before you cross the street. With a haircut like this, you could be the cause of a four-car pile-up."

"Maybe I should wear a hat."

"Don't wear a hat. Take the risk. You really look great. And listen. Next time, don't shave before you come in. I am expanding my repertoire to include the old fashioned shave. I just bought a straight razor. Stainless steel. I am talking nineteenth century now, with lather all over the floor. I've been practicing at home, on my dog. You could be my first human customer, although I might not be able to offer my usual guarantee."

Dreaming With Montalvo And Cortez

Years ago I dreamed I was a priest sailing west from Mexico with Hernando Cortez. We had been travelling for days, maybe weeks, I wasn't sure. I had lost track of time. Food was low. Many men were crazy from the voyage, lurching to their duties, crippled with diseases no one understood. Hernando was a little crazy too, giddy, drunk with the rolling seas and short rations and now the look of a coastline which he hoped would be the island his explorers had sighted years earlier. All reports had been vague. The Indians on the mainland were evasive, even when beaten. Now their coast was far behind and we had sighted a landscape such as one only sees when fingers squeeze the eyes—purple globes, and vast yellow mushrooms whose stems grow thinner, finally break from the sea's skin, turn to bubbles and float away, dissolving.

"Perhaps it is the heat," I said, "giving us mirages."

"Perhaps," said Hernando. "Perhaps not. Some things sink. Some float."

In this dream I could see the world through his eyes as well as through my own. I knew he had learned to ignore most of his apparitions—castles soaring out of the trees, the great metal ships ploughing silently toward us through a dawn fog. He could ignore the cries that came ringing across the water when we anchored close to shore, cries that echoed as if from deep alleyways. Now he tried to ignore the blue curtain that had closed in front of the ship, quivering.

He called out to his helmsman to hold the course. The ship sailed through the curtain. It parted. For an instant a solid shape appeared, tan ridges extending north as far as we could see. They wavered, broke into four pieces, four identical tan clouds floating alongside the ship.

Hernando laughed quietly and shut his eyes. "I have the perfect name for this land."

I waited, while we drew near enough to see beaches, shimmering threads of ivory. Eventually I said, "Perhaps it is the very name I myself have in mind."

"I doubt that."

"I have in fact been thinking of the name ever since we undertook this crossing."

With a sly glance Hernando said, "We will call it California."

This startled me. I turned to examine his grizzled face. Cortez was fifty. His beard was white. His eyebrows were white, as white as the deck. As white as the sky. His eyes had seen everything between Madrid and whatever land sent these drifting images toward the ship, and away from it, into the sky and plunging for the bottom. He had looked into the eyes of slaughtered Aztecs and into the mouths of men thrown overboard so their afflictions would not spread and into the wounds of Indians working under the lash to build this ship and launch it on yet another expedition, farther west. Perhaps too far. Perhaps eyes were not meant to see that much, at least not eyes that saw with anything less than absolute faith.

Hernando's eyes were filmed over now, and I saw that

in the matter of names he could no longer be trusted.
Names were permanent, and they were noted by the bishops in Madrid. They were signs of faith, new zones of spiritual power. On this voyage, each name would, in its way,
signify *my* faith, the unswerving faith that had sustained
me through a long season of trial and hardship. If we could
surround this uncharted region of the world with a rosary
of holy names, would not that be admired by the bishops in
Madrid? In Rome?

Very cautiously I said, "California? What sort of name
is that?"

Hernando roared with laughter. "It is the name of an island, Padre. Don't you read anything but scripture?"

"With all respect, Captain, new *countries* are named for
those already living there, or for something in the nature of
the land, or for the patrons of the voyage. Cities and
islands are named for saints and for symbols of the
Church. I think immediately of Santo Domingo, Guada-
lupe, Santiago, Vera Cruz . . ."

Perspiring with fever and with inspiration he interrupted this litany and rushed to his cabin. He returned,
grinning broadly, with a thick, leather-bound volume. He
flipped through to a marked page and began to read aloud:

*Now you are to hear the most extraordinary thing that ever
was heard of in any chronicles, or in the memory of
man . . .*

He made an oration of it, a call to his crewmen and soldiers to gather around. As they crept toward him, or listened from afar, too feeble to move, he continued:

*Know then that on the right hand of the Indies there is an
island called California, very near the gates of the*

> *Terrestrial Paradise, and it was peopled by black women,*
> *without any man among them . . .*

A lecherous murmur rose from the deck. I felt obliged to disapprove, and tried to frown. No one noticed. In their eyes I was invisible. One sailor called out, "Commander, if you are asking for volunteers . . ."

The murmur turned to thin, raucous cackling, silenced by Hernando's palm:

> *. . . for they lived in the fashion of Amazons. They were of*
> *strong and hardy bodies, of ardent courage and great force.*
> *Their island was the strongest in all the world, with its*
> *steep cliffs and rocky shores. Their weapons were all of*
> *gold, and so was the harness of the wild beasts which they*
> *tamed and rode. For in the whole island there was no*
> *metal but gold . . .*

At this the crew cried as one man, demanding to know the whereabouts of such a land. Hernando laughed again, his laugh outlasting their clamor. He clapped shut the novel and pointed west.

"It approaches," he shouted. "It is here!"

They pushed toward the rail, straining to peer through the glare and the dwindling mirages.

In my defeat I was petulant, yet could not conceal my fascination. "What is this book?" I whispered. "One of those . . . romances?"

Hernando shoved it toward me. "Here. Read it. It will serve you much better than the Gospels ever have. A tale of chivalry and daring called *The Adventures of Esplandian.* Montalvo is the author, Garcia Ordoñez de Montalvo. He presented this copy to me personally before we sailed from Spain. I have read it through five times now, and in all truth I wish I had another tale or two to fill these murderous nights."

I held it gingerly, fearful, and feeling like a child. "This island he mentions? Could it possibly . . . ?"

With a brief, fatherly tenderness he said, "Ah Padre, Padre, it is an invention, of course. The name. The place. All of it. A fantasy. Montalvo is as mad as the rest of us."

At the rail the men were calling out for explanations. All they could see was beach and the harsh, uninviting uplands. Cortez squinted and saw in the shade of a few low trees what he expected to see, another band of Indians, squat, murky men who stood out of the sun, too guileless or too stupid to hide. I knew he despised them for this and for the way they invariably awaited our arrival. He laughed cruelly, answering his greedy men.

"There! Right there! Don't you see?"

He pointed.

As if triggered by the raising of his arm, the distant figures sprang to life, began leaping, running in all directions. The ground around the Indians had begun to move, perhaps the mountains too. Just a shiver. I saw Hernando shake his head and blink. He was ready to dismiss that flick of the mountain's shoulder—another apparition—and he might have, were it not for the Divine radiance that had filled my face. This told him two things—I too had seen the earth move, and I understood the timing. The tremor was a signal from On High that I, the padre, could not be overlooked.

Breathing a prayer of thanks to the Almighty, I held the novel at arms length and regarded it with lofty repugnance. When I dropped it overboard, he winced but did not move. The book splashed into a small backwash the tremor had thrown out from shore, and this backwash was not lost on Hernando. It was real: a little echo of the

Heavenly warning. As he noted the rocking of his ship, his eyes told me he was ready to bargain, a renegade, but not a heretic.

"The name I was thinking of," I murmured, "is San Lucas. Saint Luke."

"A bold man," said he, "a worthy saint."

"A sounder name, wouldn't you agree, than . . ." I gestured, perhaps too arrogantly, toward the drowning volume.

"For a headland? Absolutely. I am sure that is what you had in mind. Cabo San Lucas. The Cape of Saint Luke. But for an entire island? We need something bold. We want a name that will stir the blood! And look! There! The way the natives scramble—as if to greet us!"

Hernando laughed, blinking again, to clear his head. The earth was calm, the quaking had subsided, yet the Indians still seemed out of their minds with terror and confusion. This too Cortez despised. They were always so much less than his Montalvos could conjure.

His laughter multiplied, swelled to thunder. He called out to his men, "Look! Look! They run to welcome us! Women with dark bodies! Women with no men! Is it not as I proclaimed? Is this not the isle of California?"

Some of the crew began to see it then as he described. From the rail they bellowed huzzahs and rowdy taunts. We were all yelling something—Cortez, the gaunt and tattered crew, and me, the outvoted padre, trying to remind them it was only sand, and unChristian sand at that.

"Sand and heathens!" I cried.

They didn't hear. The screech of pulleys buried my voice, as they began to lower the landing boats, scrambling for the oars, bearing Bibles and rum and the King's colors. I had no choice then but to join them. Whatever Hernando decided to call this land, a cross would have to be raised. Part of my job was to stand next to the cross.

As we pushed off from the ship, another blue curtain rose ahead of us. It hung above the beach, as wide and as blue as the sea itself. The beach began to quiver again, dividing into tiny eggs. They slid upward and under the curtain of watery blue. When they returned, they were undulating, as if alive, a long strand of egg-shaped, ivory beads. I was in the first boat, next to Hernando, and I remember the furious passion in his voice as he shouted at his rowers to pull as they had never pulled before.

Homage To The Count

The ad said IN PERSON, at THE COCOANUT GROVE, SANTA CRUZ, the one and only COUNT BASIE. We said, "We'd better go to this one. The Count is getting up there. What is he now? 70? These guys aren't going to be around forever, you know. Ellington is gone. Father Hines is gone. Eubie Blake. We better get some tickets."

It was like the old days. The semi-dark ballroom shimmered with chips of light thrown across the walls and floor from a crystal ball revolving high overhead. The floor was glossed for dancers but nobody was dancing yet, everyone crowding toward the bandstand watching the musicians settle in, waiting to pay tribute and wanting to be close enough to get the full blast from the four trombones and four trumpets and five front-row saxophones.

Back behind the dance floor a smaller crowd clung to the cocktail tables in the lounge that overlooks the beach and pier. Above the floor, others sat at the horseshoe railing, rimmed with tiny lights, like a glittering rim of boxes at the opera.

At last the curtains parted behind the bandstand, and two tall men appeared, wearing the dark suits all the musicians wore. They waited a few moments, until a head appeared between them, a shorter man, nearly bald, moving so slowly he might not have been moving at all. The tall musicians each took an arm as he inched along, down the tiers, on his painful journey toward the piano. It took four or five minutes. He too wore a dark suit, high white collar, boldly striped tie. He did not look at the crowd until he reached the grand, had one hand on it for support. Then he raised his head with a wag and a slow grin as if to say, "That wasn't as bad as I thought it was going to be." The grin was a relief. We began to applaud, a ripple that swelled to an ovation.

"He's 79," I heard a woman say. "I read in the paper he's had arthritis, diabetes, two heart attacks."

His face was thinner than the photo in the ad, which had caught him in his heyday, wearing the jaunty skipper's cap. In the spotlight his skimpy hair was a gray shadow across the scalp. Under the dark skin, his face looked gray. It was the showman's smile and the sly glance that told you this was The Count, together with the music that burst forth as he nodded his venerable head—a three-tiered chorus of brass and reeds filling the Grove with the unmistakable sound that made him the king-daddy of big-band swing. Yes, here it came, the full-bodied, bass-powered locomotive of swing, kept on track by the elegant righthand that knows precisely how, with one cluster of high-register bluesy notes, to maintain command. . . .

But wait a minute. Something was missing. What was it? I listened. It was just that: the famous Basie right hand. I wasn't hearing it. What happened? He was sitting there. He was nodding and smiling like a piano player. The band sounded great, and it was undeniably the Basie band playing in the Basie style. Maybe the piano mike was out.

I listened closely to another number, then walked around to the far side of the stand. Through the packed crowd I found a sight line and saw that he was not playing. As the next tune began, his hands rested on the keys like empty gloves. From time to time a finger pushed a key, but so languidly it made no sound. He watched his band with a proprietary eye, nodding slow approval as a soloist left the fore-stage mike, sometimes grinning toward the bass man as if they shared some secret. He reached for a sheet of music and moved it from the top of the piano to the little shelf in front of him. But he wasn't playing. He wasn't even trying to fake it.

I felt cheated. The elegant touch of that righthand had always been Basie's signature, those few well-chosen notes plucked from a melody line, surrounded with tempo, surrounded with space. When he finally tried to end one number with his traditional punctuation, I realized why the piano mike had been turned down close to zero. The notes were in place, but the strength was gone, the agility was gone. I almost left the ballroom then, overwhelmed with sadness and grief for the man propped up there on the stage, a living legend, who could still talk but who could no longer walk or do what he was famous for.

I didn't leave, because the band had a holding power of its own. Soon I had stopped paying such close attention to Basie. With or without his piano they were so tight they cast a spell and carried me away, bass, drums, thirteen sidemen dressed like bank vice presidents, each a master of his instrument, and bringing that mastery to the Basie sound, faithful to it all night long: *"Indian Summer," "Sunny Side of The Street," "Easy Living," "Our Love is Here to Stay."* At one point three sax players doubled on flutes to accent a muted trumpet solo in just the way his piano used to do. It was stirring. It was classic. It was danceable. You had to dance. And every step was a little celebration, just as every drum roll was a tribute to the style and influence of this man whose playing and dancing days were over.

I remembered seeing a Buddhist holy man called the Gyalwa Karmapa at the Civic Auditorium, passing through Santa Cruz on his way to Nirvana, back in 1980. He too had packed the place and had reached an age where he had to be helped up the stairs, and he too was surrounded by musicians, playing high temple music from Tibet. All the Karmapa did was recline on the stage, on a throne-like couch in his garments, while eight hundred of us passed one by one in front of him to receive a blessing. He smiled and his eyes filled with a glowing ease, and if you believed that he embodied spiritual truth, it was enough just to be in his presence. You walked out of the Civic feeling blessed.

So it was with Basie. If there is a temple music in America, he has to be listed among its primary sources, along with those other performer/heroes of his generation, vocalists and hornmen and piano players who started recording in the 1920s—Ellington, Louis Armstrong, Benny Goodman, Bessie Smith, Mildred Bailey, Glenn Miller, Fats Waller. As of that night Basie was still among the few survivors. During the first set he said, with a smile that was part showbiz and part elder statesman and part saint, "It's good to be here with you . . . one more time." The immortal righthand that gave us *"Take the A Train"* and *"Red Bank Boogie"* lay at rest on the keyboard. The eyes and the smile were saying, "It will be a miracle if I pass this way again."

It could have been a mushy, sentimental moment. But the Count did not linger there. He had not lost his sense of timing. His glance toward the rhythm section triggered a walking bass line that brought four trombone players to their feet. Gutsy brass filled the ballroom, while eager dancers moved out among the swirling chips of light.

The Men In My Life

I wish I was in the land of cotton.
Oldtimes there are not forgotten . . .
Dixie (1859), by Daniel Decatur Emmett

In 1809 my great-great-great-great grandfather left Buncombe County, North Carolina, and crossed over the Ap-
palachians into central Tennessee. I have thought a lot
about that trip. Of the numerous trips it has taken to bring
my family—that is, the handful of us scattered along this
coastline—from the eastern edge of the continent to the
western edge, that one looms largest in my imagination. I
cannot say it looms large in memory. No one now living
knows much at all about it, nor have I heard it talked
about or seen anything written about it, apart from the
dates and the names of counties, and the prices he paid for
a couple of pieces of land, and the name of his wife, Tem-
perance, the names of their four sons, Gideon, Louis,
Reuben, Nathan, and their one daughter, Elinder.

His name was Noble Bouldin, a church-going farmer
who came from a long line of farmers, as far back as lin-
eage can be traced. The first Bouldin to cross the Atlantic,
they say, was a fellow named Thomas, a Warwickshire

131

yeoman who landed at Jamestown in 1610 and quickly acquired some land along the James River. Perhaps he was the original immigrant ancestor. If not, there was another Bouldin, sooner or later, very much like him, who carried the seed, and Virginia was the homeland for almost two hundred years, until after the Revolutionary War, when the west began to beckon, the west, at the turn of that century, being Ohio, Kentucky, Tennessee.

In those days nothing happened suddenly. A family on the move might stop a while along the trail, set up a cabin and clear a piece of land, as Noble did, in 1803 or thereabouts. He paid a hundred dollars for fifty acres, between the Blue Ridge Mountains and The Great Smokies and worked it for a couple of years, no doubt picking up scraps of information here and there about what lay beyond the peaks in the distance.

Perhaps he made the next trip alone, the first time, scouting ahead before bringing his family farther than most white Americans had ever travelled and into territory few had ever seen. Perhaps it took a couple of weeks, or a month, with long days of solitary riding, during which he missed his wife and children, but also savored the solitude and the daily discovery of new terrain. On one such morning he may have got an early start and reached a ridge top just as the sun rose behind him, adding sudden clarity and sharp shadows to the rippling landscape, causing his heart to swell and his skin to prickle and his blood to run. He may have shouted something then, one long syllable of exultation.

Or perhaps not. Perhaps he was a born slob, unmoved by natural wonders, insensitive to color and light, and concerned only with grabbing the best piece of land he could find before someone else got hold of it. Maybe he was an ignorant, stubborn, hot-headed redneck, a rifle-toting hillbilly racist from North Carolina. But I prefer not to re-

member him that way. I prefer to dwell on his name—
Noble—and to look in his farmer's heart for signs of noble
character. I prefer to see him on the ridge top at dawn, like
a wolf in the wilderness, celebrating with his voice, celebrating the miracle of his own life.

However it happened, he must have liked what he saw
or had heard about. According to Court House records, he
sold his Buncombe County acreage for a two hundred dollar profit. Then he packed up his family and all their
worldly goods and continued west. There were tools to
carry, a plough, knives and rifles, a Bible or two, a fiddle.
Noble was in his thirties then, halfway through the Appa-
lachians and halfway through his life. I see him wearing a
hat like the one Walt Whitman wore for the frontispiece to
Leaves of Grass, a dark and wide-brimmed hat, tipped back.
No one knows what he looked like. He passed away before
cameras came along. I can only speculate, and hope, that
he resembled Whitman, with that kind of questioning eye,
the trimmed beard showing some gray, and the top button of his long johns showing underneath the open-neck
shirt.

He would be walking in front of a horse, and Temper-
ance would be riding, in order to hold and nurse the new-
born daughter. There were other horses, perhaps a wagon
or two, perhaps not. It was spring, and the ground was
cool and damp, but no longer muddy, and by the summer
of 1809 they had staked out a Tennessee homestead, in
Warren County, near the banks of the Collins River.

After that, one thing led to another. Noble had already
begat Gideon, who was thirteen when they made this journey. Gideon eventually built a house right on the county
line, making it possible, so I have heard, to leave Warren
County and cross over into Van Buren County just by
stepping from the parlor into the kitchen.

In 1831 Gideon begat Montesque, the fifth of his ten children and my great-great grandfather, naming him after the 18th century French philosopher. I will defend the mountainized spelling of this name the same way George Hearst once defended himself at the California Democratic Convention. The rambunctious, self-made millionaire father of William Randolph Hearst, George was hoping to be nominated for governor. One of his opponents had accused him of being so ignorant he had spelled the word bird, b-u-r-d. "If b-u-r-d does not spell bird," Hearst asked his fellow delegates, "just what in the hell *does* it spell?"

If M-o-n-t-e-s-q-u-e does not spell Montesquieu, what else in the world *could* it spell?

This fellow did two things that linger in the family memory. 1. Sometime before the Civil War he left the flat farm lands his grandfather and father had settled and worked, and he moved up onto the nearby Cumberland Plateau. In a region called Pleasant Hill he built a two-story house out of axe-hewn logs and began to raise his family. 2. When the war came along he did not fight for the South, as several of his brothers did. Montesque fought for the North. Or so goes the official version of that era—the official version being what I first heard from my grandmother, as she passed her memories on, during the years when I was growing up in San Francisco. Back in 1969, however, when I made my one and only pilgrimage into the Cumberlands to look up some of the surviving relatives, looking for the grandads and great-grandads I might have known, I heard another version, and one that appealed to me a lot more.

One of Montesque's grandsons was still alive, an aging cousin thrice removed, who had spent his whole life in those mountains, farming mostly. At eighty he was erect and spry and vigorous, wore a twill shirt, coveralls. He felt a special bond with Montesque, since he was the only one in the family, or in the entire world, for that matter, to inherit the name. I should say, he *almost* inherited the name. When it crossed the Atlantic, from Paris to Van Buren County, in the 1830s, two letters had fallen out, like teeth. And somewhere between the generations, a consonant had disappeared, so that this eighty-year-old cousin of mine had ended up with a name that is surely unique in the long history of French-speakers taking liberties with English and English-speakers getting even by taking liberties with French. His given name was *Montacue*.

We were in the front room of his old frame house in the little town of Spencer, Tennessee, sitting in two straight-backed chairs, when I asked him about this spelling. He shook his silvered head in true wonder.

"It's always mystified me," he said, "how a whole letter could get lost like that. When I was born, grandad was still alive and sure must a knowed how to say his own name. It aint like people up here got somethin so big caught between their teeth, they're afraid to let some air through. I guess that ol *S* just dropped out of sight about like the way grandad did during the war."

"Which war was that?" I said.

"*The* war," he said.

"I heard somewhere that he fought for the North."

"Nope. He never fought for the North. Not my grandad. Not Montesque Bouldin."

"That means he must have fought for the South."

"Nope."

Again he shook his head, not with wonder now, but with purpose and what looked like the beginning of a grin. "He didn't fight for the South neither."

"Well then, what did he do during the war?"

The craggy face opened. The eyes gleamed with

pleasure. "Far as I know, he didn't fight for nobody. He just hid out til the whole thing was over."

"Hid out?"

"Hunted. Kept to himself. Stayed off the roads. Wasn't nobody goin to find a person up here who didn't want to be found. Wasn't nobody goin to come lookin for him anyhow. In these mountains. A hunderd years ago. There's places I could show you right now, you could have all to yourself for six or seven months. You take where I grew up, over there toward Pleasant Hill, where grandad built his log house. You can't even git in there now. I don't know if I could show you how to *start* gittin in there, it's all so growed over."

As he talked, I was thinking, That guy sounds like my kind of ancestor. Not only was he named for an eminent man of letters, he seemed to have a mind of his own. There are some, I suppose—other cousins, on other branches of the family tree—who would call it sloth and cowardice, not to have fought for one side or the other, when his own brothers were out there somewhere slogging through the mud and gunsmoke of the 1860s. But Montesque's grandson obviously didn't see it that way. Nor did I, the great-great-grandson, dreaming of hide-outs.

As we sat there, grinning about this forerunner we had in common, and the memory of his independent spirit, I began to dwell on the episode, as I had long dwelled upon the trans-Appalachian passage. I began to see those mountains from high altitude, as if hovering in a hot-air balloon, and high enough to observe uncountable puffs of smoke rising from invisible rifle barrels far to the north and far to the south, a wide circle of silent puffs and cannon clouds. In the center, surrounded by forest, there is a softer puff, a misty cloud rising at the base of a mountain waterfall, and Montesque is standing there in his boots and his heavy trousers.

Next to him stands a little girl. She is six years old, already lean and tough-limbed, tough as hickory, the way she will be throughout her life. Her name is Arminda, though he calls her Mindy, his oldest and favorite daughter, who has just hiked two miles through the trees to bring him a pail of food. The pail is sitting on a rock, and she is looking at it because the hike has made her hungry, hungrier than usual. She is hungry all the time. She says, "You gonna eat pretty soon, pa?" And he says, "Fore long." And she says, "When you comin home?" And he says, "You miss me, darlin?"

"Mama says to tell you the soldiers come and gone and they didn't git near our place."

"Did you see em?"

"Mama says they look so sick and raggedy she doesn't believe they'll ever hike through these woods again. Or any other woods."

"Well, that's real good news, darlin. Now what we got to eat in that bucket?"

"It's only cornbread, pa. Mama says we just about run out of everything else."

"You tell your mama there is a bear likes to wander down to the far end of this here pool every evenin about sundown, and it won't be long fore he takes his last drink a water."

"You gonna shoot him, pa?"

"I might. Or I might just sneak up behind him and catch him by the neck and stick his head under the waterfall just like I'm gonna do you," grabbing her lightly then, lifting her under the skinny arms to swing her out over the pool, while she squeals with fearful delight.

Later, while they are hunkered down in the grass, breaking off chunks of cornbread, she says, "Pa?"

Through his mouthful he grunts, "Yunnh?"

"Can I stay here with you?"

He chews a while and looks at her and looks away and says, "No darlin. Mama needs you back home. And I'll be back home fore you know it. You tell her I said that too."

And much later, while she trots through the twilight forest, to make it home before dark, she is already remembering that lift over the water as if it happened long long ago, the ecstasy of it, as the man in her life, the one she loves more than any other, lifts her up and swings her around and out, toward misty plumes and the plummeting rush of white. It seems to last forever. And yet it ends too soon, too soon . . .

Or maybe this little meeting of the father and the daughter did not register deeply at all. Maybe it was just another day in the long months of days when he was laying low. I am only guessing here, a grandson-at-large searching for his past, making it up as I go along, searching for some way to account for the look in her eyes in the earliest photo of Arminda I have seen, taken right at the turn of the century. Forty years and nine children later, her stern and weathered face says, "Nothing lasts forever," and "Everything lasts too long."

*

Yes, Noble begat Gideon. And Gideon begat Montesque. And Montesque begat seven sons and daughters, among them Arminda, who was my great-grandmother, born in that two-story house at Pleasant Hill. Around the age of twenty-two she married into another mountain clan, Irish in origin, if you trace it back far enough, another line of farmers and smalltime landholders who had arrived in Tennessee by way of North Carolina. Her husband's name was James Wiley Gulley. He too is in that turn-of-the-century photo, slouched next to her, and I am sure he contributed something to the look on Arminda's face, as husbands always do. She was well past forty by that time. She looks past sixty, sitting up straight, with her knees together, underneath the full-length, neck-to-shoetops dress. Her lips are pressed tight, her hair is pulled tight against her temples. Her eyes are formidable, challenging, as if this camera is not to be trusted.

Her husband's eyes are slant-browed, seemingly at ease. He is leaning on the chair arm, with knees apart, wearing jacket and vest, but no tie. His hair is uncombed. Perhaps he has been drinking. It has always looked that way to me. This was their first and only family portrait. If he'd had a couple of quick ones while they were setting up the shot, I wouldn't have held it against him, being the father of nine children, in those times, which were hard times all across the land and particularly in the south. Behind him stands his oldest daughter, who has just turned twenty. On his knee he holds a son who looks to be about three, while Arminda holds their youngest, a girl not yet a year old.

It must have been a madhouse getting everyone dressed and in position for this picture, which represents about ten seconds in their combined years on earth. The camera clicks, and a moment later the faces unfreeze, a chair scoots back, the talk begins, as the son-in-law standing in the back row rips loose the chafing, high starched collar, and as great-grandma breaks out the corncob pipe she smoked. What I wish for here is a movie of the day they took this portrait, an hour before and an hour afterward, with all the grunts and belches and the curling smoke. And yet this frozen moment captures something essential, bearing out everything else I have heard about these two great-grandparents of mine. Unbending, severe, Arminda was the stronger, the family rudder, and J.W. was the lovable ne'er-do-well, a singer, a joker, a man "with a long streak of fun in him," as I heard one old nephew say.

Perhaps it was the inclination of Arminda, the oldest daughter, to take command of things, and the inclination of James Wiley, who had older brothers, to let her do just that. Or perhaps it was something about the characters of their two clans. The Bouldins tend to be built like trees, ramrod straight, both men and women, and among themselves they make remarks about the Gulleys, as people do—families, clans, tribes, nations—who have intermingled through the years. The remarks are made lightly, in intimate jest. The receding chins of certain Gulley men, I have heard it said, suggest uncertainty of purpose. In a friendly and kidding sort of way someone will point to a small, fenced and long-untended graveyard where Gulleys were buried, until it was abruptly closed back in 1912. The last grave dug there was filling up with water faster than the gravediggers could bail it out—a sign of the high water table at that particular spot, and also an example of the unfortunate choices Gulleys tend to make.

On the other hand, it may be that my grandmother was right when she said the Union Army left on her father a lasting mark, and that this is somehow the key to his character. She grew up listening to his tirades about Yankees. She often said he had re-fought the Civil War every day of his adult life. Too young to enlist, he was old enough to remember the day a detachment of Union soldiers appeared in their yard. He was ten at the time. His father and older brothers were off somewhere fighting on the Confederate side and had left young Jim behind to take care of his mama and be the man of the family. She was in labor, so the story goes, when these barbarian northerners arrived at the farm, like locusts, and left with every live animal and every scrap of food, including a stash of turnips and potatoes Jim had buried.

He never forgave them for what they did that day, stripping the farm while his mother lay there crying out with labor pains. The *them* he never forgave included that small band of soldiers, together with all officers and enlisted men in the entire Union Army, and every man, woman and child who happened to live north of the Mason-Dixon line. In later years some of his grandchildren would deliberately take the northern side in the endless debate, just to get him started. They would prod him to tell that story again, hoping he would follow it with other tales of Yankee treachery and deceit and end up singing *Dixie*, his favorite song. (He did not know and so was never troubled by the strange irony that this Confederate call to battle had been written in New York City by a composer from Ohio):

> Then I wish I was in Dixie. Hooray! Hooray!
> In Dixieland I'll take my stand
> To live and die in Dixie . . .

That is how my grandmother liked to remember him, sitting on the front porch in Huntsville, Alabama, singing gospel songs or patriotic songs about the south.

Maybe this is why he chose to move his family out of the mountains and into a mill town in another state—to put a hundred and fifty more miles between himself and the hated north. Or maybe it was that decade's depression, and the near worthlessness of cash crops, that decided him to give up trying to scrape a living from his fifty acres outside Spencer. Or maybe it was some old restlessness in the blood that sent him in search of travelling money, when he agreed to team up with a brother-in-law and pick a large orchard somewhere down the hillside, on Bouldin land. These two men moved their families into a house near the orchard, for a month of picking and peeling and slicing and drying. They built two drying kilns right there and came up with sixteen hundred pounds of produce, which netted Jim Gulley about forty-eight dollars. With that and a covered wagon, he and Arminda and their eight kids set out for Alabama. They kept fifty pounds of dried apples to eat along the way and carried fifty pounds of fresh apples to trade for other food. It took them a week to make the trip, which is not quite as fast as a person on foot could have walked it.

I see Jim in his coveralls, hunched above the reins. He does not hear the squabble breaking out amongst the kids crammed in behind him, nor does he notice the line of brown spittle staining his beard. He is chewing tobacco and thinking of their next stop, when he can step behind the widest tree and take a pull from the flask he has hidden somewhere on board, and he is dreaming the dream you always dream when you pull up stakes, of another start, or an easier life, or at the very least another way of doing things.

His family had been in Tennessee about sixty years. Arminda's had been there for ninety. In our patchwork legend, this wagonload of kids rolling south over rocky roads at the speed of three miles per hour is remembered as a kind of exodus from the homeland, the wagon pulled by donkeys and covered with bedsheets stretched over curving hickory staves.

Their destination, their Mecca, their Jerusalem, their Silicon Valley, was the Huntsville of the 1890s, a town which had recently become a new industrial center, fueled with Yankee money and drawing country people from all directions, to work in the textile mills. The shifts were long, and the pay was low (fifty cents a night, my grandmother told me). But the work was steady, and a man with a big family was considered a lucky man indeed, in those pre-child-labor-law days, when anyone ten years and older was employable.

Jim Gulley soon had five of his children drawing wages, though he himself never did go to work in the mills. He took odd jobs around town, when the spirit moved him, and delivered lunches to his bread-winning crew, then tended to hang around the mill, ostensibly to make sure they behaved themselves. More likely he was hanging out with his cronies, other fathers-on-the-loose with other lunches to deliver. He was in his mid-40s then, at a time when the average lifespan was about 42. Maybe he figured he had already outlived his generation and paid his dues and earned a rest, and what were children for anyhow, if not to comfort and sustain a man through his autumn years. Or maybe it was true, what his ancient nephews cackled about when I met them in Tennessee in 1969.

"Don't you know that's why he went on down to Huntsville in the first place?" one of them told me with a wink. "If I'd a had that many young-uns, I'd a done the same. Ol Jim, he was lazy, but wasn't dumb. And he never wore a long face neither. Wasn't nothin could get him down. I remember the time him and Bud Bouldin picked that orchard clean and dried all them apples. Jim was working overtime there for a spell, but he already knew he was on his way offa this mountain, ya see. He was whistlin all day long and singin so loud you could hear him clear to Memphis."

*

That formal family portrait was taken on the front porch in Huntsville, four or five years after they had settled in. It hangs now in my living room here in Santa Cruz, where I pass it several times a day, a portal, an opening into a long-gone world. I think of it as a door that swings two ways, into the past and into the future. The year was 1901, the threshold of the 20th century. These great-grandparents,

Jim and Arminda, could be any of the ancestors of the previous two hundred years. Their faces, their body angles,
their clothes are of an older time. But that young girl at the
far right, the one with the dark hair piled high, rolled and
shining, with the thoughtful and sadly burdened eyes, she
is my grandmother, Nora Alda Belle Gulley. Of the dozen
people in this photo she will be the only one to continue the
journey to the continent's farthest edge.

She is thirteen here, but like her mother, she looks much
older. She is not a schoolgirl and never will be. She has already put in three years of ten-hour shifts at the cotton
mill. She has her mother's long limbs and wears the same
kind of dress, sleeves to the wrist, collar to the chin, hem to
the floor, everything covered but the hands and the head.

She has her father's slant-browed eyes, and at thirteen
she is showing at least one of his traits: she is not cooperat-
ing. In this photo she is the only one not gazing at the camera. She has glanced away. Perhaps a young man on
horseback has just trotted around the corner, though I
doubt it. The eyes don't seem aimed at anything specific.
While her body sits on the porch, her mind is elsewhere.
Knowing how her life turned out, I can read into her look
the wistful foreknowledge of the man who will one day en-
tice her, and father her children, and then disappear, the
reluctant husband, the main man in her life, and a man in
mine too, though I never met him, the grandfather who
covered his tracks.

This is what I see in those young/old eyes. Already she is
watching him walk away.

His name was Eddie Wilson, a young mill hand from
Danville, Virginia, or so he claimed, who moved into their
neighborhood in 1909 or 1910. So little is known about this
fellow I call him Elusive Eddie. He had black hair and blue
eyes, and like Jim Gulley he was a sometime singer who

appreciated good singing when he heard it. Sixty years later I met a woman in Huntsville who said she once had a crush on Eddie. A few years younger than my grand-mother, she evidently had watched their courtship with teenage jealousy.

"In the evenin, after work," she told me, "if it was warm, Nora would sit out there on the porch with her guitar and sing *Red River Valley*, and Eddie would yell across the street, 'You'd break the heart of any boy in Alabama!'"

Eddie too played guitar, and mentioned once that he had some Cherokee blood. He also liked to pick clover on the way to the mill and make up songs about it.

Or so I've been told.

Everything is vague, except the marriage date, 1910, and the fact that he was gone by the time my mother was born, and the huge silence that later surrounded his mem-ory. Though family meant more to Nora than anything but heaven itself, she would never talk about this man who was the only man she married and the only man she dated after the age of twenty-two. Eventually he wrote and told her he had joined the army. A while later she sent him a photo of their baby girl. He then wrote from Griffin, Georgia, beg-ging to come back. It was the only letter of his she kept, and she kept it hidden from the world until she was almost eighty.

"My dearest little wife . . ." it begins.

Three years after he had disappeared, he returned to Huntsville and in due time my uncle was born. But by then, Elusive Eddie was gone again, heading to Virginia, he said as he left, to borrow some money to put down on their house.

One of Nora's younger sisters witnessed this farewell and remembered her parting words to him.

"Eddie," Nora said, "as sure as we're standin on the ground, I am never gonna see you again."

"I'm comin back as quick as I can," said Eddie. "I swear it."

She may have heard from him after that, but she burned all the letters. No photos have survived, and no information at all after 1923, which was the last time anyone remembers hearing he might have been spotted. It was near Danville. Many years later the brother of a friend of the family recalled seeing him in a cotton mill. "How you doin, Eddie?" he called out, "Long time, no see." But this fellow in his 30s who resembled Eddie and moved like Eddie and was back at Eddie's original line of work, told this brother of a friend of the family that he must be mistaken. The next day he had checked out of the mill, whoever he was, moving on. Where to? No one knows? Where from? We can only guess. Any relatives? None to speak of. A letter he had supposedly written to a sister, before he married Nora, came back to Huntsville unopened. Forty-five years later a phone-book poll of all the Wilsons in the Danville area turned up no leads. Once or twice Nora asked him to tell her the story of his life, but he never got around to it. In that one letter she saved, he wrote:

> You said tell you what I had bin doing these long
> yeares well darling you no that would fill a com-
> mon size book and I will tell you all about it
> when I come . . .

She was 79 when she finally dug out these pages and showed them to me, the grandson with a taste for history, pressing for evidence. Though she knew exactly where the letter was, she had not looked at it for decades. She put on her glasses and read it aloud, while color rose into her cheeks. She began to cry. My mother was there, and she too began to cry at the sound of this message from the longlost father. We all cried at the words rising out of his fifty-year silence. For me, it was the first real proof of his existence. Until then I'd had nothing to validate him, nothing as solid as a letter written by hand, on folded and fragile paper, in purple ink. Now his words, the voice of the missing grandfather, were coming from her throat, like the disembodied words a medium pulls out of thin air.

*

With money saved from her years of paychecks, Nora went ahead and bought a house in Huntsville, by that time knowing two things for sure: she wanted to make a home for her kids, but she did not want them growing up in the mills. When an older brother moved to Texas, in search of a drier climate for his wife's lungs, Nora soon followed, sold her house, put the equity into a quarter-section of the Texas panhandle, and went back to the farming life she had known as a young girl in Tennessee. Before long half her family had made this move, other brothers and sisters, and Jim and Arminda, who spent their final years out there.

On her deathbed, in 1926, Arminda summoned her grandchildren one at a time. My mother was fifteen then and remembers the last words she heard from this fierce-eyed woman born in a log house before the Civil War.

"Loretta," she said, "don't you never go ridin alone in a car with a man."

"I sure won't, grandma," my mother said, thinking 'Not if I can help it anyway.' And she may actually have tried, for a while, to follow this advice. But by that time, as we know, the world was filling up with cars. A few years later she was riding alone in one with my father, as they left Texas together, heading west and bound for California.

Nora eventually leased the farm and followed her daughter. She lived with us or near us, in San Francisco and later in Santa Clara Valley, for the rest of her life. She always considered herself a widow and tended to dress that way. In her view, Eddie was dead and gone. Yet she kept his name, and that in itself gave him a ghostly presence during the years of my growing up.

She had come west without a man, but I realize now how many she brought with her. She was a channel for all the southern names and places. She talked about life "up on the mountain," as if the mountain were rising right outside the window, between our house and Golden Gate Park. She sang songs her dad learned when he was young, and some of them were playful, like *The Crawdad Song*:

> Yonder come a man with a sack on his back,
>   honey.
> Yonder come a man with a sack on his back,
>   babe.
> Yonder come a man with a sack on his back,
> Got more crawdads than he can pack, honey,
>   baby mine.

Others had a haunting and medieval sound, and years later I would learn, via the F. J. Child collection of *English and Scottish Popular Ballads,* that she was puttering around our kitchen humming versions of tunes that had crossed the Atlantic two hundred years earlier, to be carried into the Cumberlands along with the rifles and the plough:

> There were three crows up in a tree,
> and they were as black as black could be.

With a humble bumble snigger-eye grinner
snooze-eye rinktum boozer.

One of those crows said to his mate,
'What we gonna do for grub to eat?'
With a humble bumble snigger-eye grinner
snooze-eye rinktum boozer.

She was the channel for ballads, for voices, for all these an-
cestral details that otherwise might have been lost to me.
She also passed on a way of thinking about ancestry that is
essentially Biblical, and patriarchal. After the first few ele-
mentary grades, she had no more formal education. But
she studied the Bible every day. It was her source and ref-
erence, her solace and inspiration. Wanting to transmit the
best of what she knew and believed, Nora would read
aloud at night from the Old Testament. The stories in *Gene-*
sis had a special appeal for her. With that soft, grandmoth-
erly, mountain voice she often read aloud from *Genesis*:

And Enoch lived sixty-five years
and begat Methusaleh . . .

And Methusaleh lived a hundred and
eighty-seven years and begat Lamech . . .

And Lamech lived a hundred and eighty-two
years and begat a son, and he called
his name Noah . . .

And Noah was five hundred years old, and
he begat Shem, Ham and Japheth . . .

Eight or ten years of this, when you are young and impres-
sionable, can have a powerful effect. The elegant ring of
the King James Version itself can work a spell on you. It
seeps into your blood and into your way of measuring time

and charting a family's path. Maybe this is why the missing grandfather came to preoccupy me. There was a place in the genealogy and in the nervous system crying out to be filled. And maybe this is why I travelled back to the homelands in 1969, in search of patriarchs.

Or maybe it was simpler than that. I had lived with both my grandmothers. They both came west to spend time with us. Having known them and their unconditional love, I had no need to go looking for replacements. But the grandfathers were both out of reach. Elusive Eddie had closed the door behind him, while the grandad on my father's side had passed away in Texas before I was old enough to make that kind of trip. I see now how consistently I have been drawn to elderly men. I never went looking for a father figure, because my dad was always there. He came home every night. But I have sought out grandfatherly men, elders who seem to carry in their eyes and in their faces some knowledge of ancient times.

Among the numerous old Bouldins and Gulleys I met during that pilgrimage to Tennessee and Alabama, one drew me more than all the others. He seemed to be the elder I had come searching for. It was old Montacue, my great-grandmother's nephew, my grandmother's first cousin, a man of her age, who had never left Van Buren County. He welcomed me as if we had known each other for a lifetime. Perhaps we had. I recognized him instantly and recognized someone in myself, the subsistence farmer I might have been, or could have been.

He led me to the shed outside his house where all the canned goods were stored on shelves, sealed Mason jars filled with fruits and vegetables. He handed me a quart of applesauce, just like Nora would have done, if I had come visiting, pressing it on me, and then a quart of string beans striped with sliced pimentoes. As he was reaching toward a pint of jelly, I protested. I was flying, I told him, and my carry-on luggage was already crammed full. He refused to hear this remark. Pushing the third jar into my arms, he nodded toward the string beans and looked at me with a kind of relentless, stubborn generosity. "Them Kentucky Wonders'll surprise ya, I guarantee it. They're gonna taste mighty good when you git home."

We walked out into his small orchard, where the last yellow leaves of autumn hung on the apple trees. I have a photo of the two of us standing among the leaves, beyond his white frame house. Gazing at it now I see that he looked exactly the way I always wanted a grandad to look, in his coveralls, his twill shirt, his ruddy cheeks, his silvered hair. He was taller than I am, and that too felt good, to have a grandad you can physcially look up to, even at age eighty.

*

I idealize him, of course. I idealize them all. Having met him and some others of his generation only once, I can fill in most of the rest myself, create my own ancestry. We have to do a lot of that, in any event. We get some names and dates, if we are lucky, whatever trickles toward our own time. But most of it is lost. The number of teeth old Montacue had at sixty; what he thought at age twenty-five walking alone behind his mule; what he used to say when he made love, or what he failed to say—these are the details you have to fill in for yourself. It makes you wonder if there is any real difference between the making of your family's past and the making of fiction. In either case a process of very careful selection is at work.

In the paragraph above, for instance, I mention his coveralls and his ruddy cheeks. I left out his arthritic knuckles. Why? Maybe I forgot. Maybe I didn't want to go into it.

Maybe I am superstitious, afraid that mentioning a cousin's arthritis will have an effect on my own knuckles later on.

That is just one example. The process of selection is a process of invention. Take Montesque Bouldin, and the two extant versions of his allegiance during the Civil War. Not only do I choose to believe what his grandson told me, I choose to see his non-combat record as honorable behaviour, another form of heroism. Or take Noble, a fellow from Virginia, who passed through North Carolina on his way to Tennessee. Why start with him? Somewhere back there I had thirty-one other great-great-great-great grandfathers of more or less his age. Anyone of them could serve as progenitor. But who were they? What were their names, their jobs, their passions? Some were Scots, some were German, some were Cherokee, some were Louisiana French, with maybe a little Cajun blending in. But who knows how much? What role models might they have offered, what identity supports? I'll never find out. They are invisible now, or receding fast, whereas Noble is remembered because the Bouldins happened to be ardent record keepers and bearers of the family flame, and because Nora came west with her memories, and because she liked to talk.

My father's mother didn't talk as much, or know as much. On his side the family memory gets very dim around 1900. And I don't really mind. Thirty-two great-great-great-great grandfathers is probably more than I could deal with. One is plenty, although in truth I could have let Noble join the others. I could have chosen to forget him. He just happens to appeal to me. He is a gift from my grandmother, one I happily accept. So it is with all these ancestors. They create me. I create them. We give each other life.

Take Elusive Eddie, the man who passed through Huntsville on his way to who knows where. I will never be able to let him go. I still try to picture him, and when I do the picture is not black-and-white. The years before the First World War were lemon-tinted years, and grandmother's long dress touches the grass, with her hair piled high and her waist cinched tight, as her beau departs, moving off into thick sunlight. They are in a park in Alabama, beside a pavilion where a brass band plays. I see light glinting off the tuba, the trombone, playing background music for a distant voice, a young woman's plaintive voice, half humming, half singing.

Her arm lifts to shade her eyes, taffeta crinkling at the elbow. It is her one good dress, saved for rare occasions, for this Saturday stroll, only to find herself watching him leave, his slow-motion exit across the shimmering grass, his reckless boater tipped, his custard trousers lost in the glare off the lake, while she hums and sings:

> Man fell down and bust that sack, honey.
> Man fell down and bust that sack, babe.
> Man fell down and bust that sack,
> Just watch them crawdads backin back . . .

She watches with eyes that were shaped at birth to expect this and every other burden, and yet in all these years he has not gone twenty paces, light so thick and luminous how can anyone escape.

Elegy
(Written At The County
Junkyard)

At the county dump I am throwing away my father. His old paint rags, and stumps of brushes. Color catalogues. The caked leather suitcase he used for so many years carrying small tools and tiny jars of his trade, suitcase so cracked and bent and buckle-ripped it's no good for anything now, not even what he used it for. I start to toss it on top of the brushes and the rags, but hesitate, toss instead the five-gallon drums that once held primer. He stacked them against one wall of his shop, for nothing, kept dozens more than he'd ever use. Around these fall the ointments from his medicine chest. And cracked galoshes, filled with dust, as if in his closet it has been raining dust for years. And magazines. His fishing hat. Notes to himself:

> *Fix window.*
> *Grease car.*
> *Call Ed*
> *Call Harlow about job*

Bents nails in a jar, rolls of old wire, pipe sections, fiddle he always intended to mend, embossed cards some salesman left, old paid bills, check stubs, pencils his teeth chewed.

Ragtaggle bits of this and that he touched, stacked, stored, useless to anyone but him, and he's gone now, so toss it all out there among the refrigerators and lettuce leaves and seven hundred truck tires, busted sofas, flower pots, and grass from the overgrown gardens of every household. Into it I throw my father, saving for last that suitcase of his, first seen twenty years back, and old then, the first day he took me out on a job, pair of his spattered overalls to wear, rolled thick at the cuff, and Sherwin-Williams white billcap, and us two squatting while he unbuckles the case and touches dark labels of pigment tubes, deciding something.

Crusted with splats of seventy colors now, lid corners split as if somebody sat on it. The ragged straps dangle. One shred of leather holds the chromium buckle, yet the buckle itself hasn't worn much at all, still catches the sun, where paint doesn't cover it, relic from those days before things tarnished in a week.

One last glance. By five tonight it'll be gone for good, when the bulldozer comes around to shove it over the side with the rest of today's arms and toes and parts of hearts.

"What're ya gonna do, dad?"

He doesn't answer. He never answers, as if it offends him to be interrupted. And I always wait, as if all those previous silences were exceptions, and this time he will turn and speak. It's a big reason for coming along this morning, the chance that out here on the job something might pass between us. I would never have been able to describe it ahead of time, but . . . something.

I wait and watch two minutes of puckering lips and long slow blinks while he studies the labels, then selects one tube, smudged and wrinkled, unscrews its top and squeezes out a little on his fingertips.

Five feet away a canvas dropcloth covers a few square

yards of hardwood floor. I follow him to a five-gallon drum he's mixing paint in. A narrow stick of plywood holds the color he's shooting for—pale pale green. He's proud of his eye, his knack for fiquring just how pale this green will be when it's dry. Squeeze a green strip from the tube and stir it in, wide easy stirs while the green spreads out like taffy strips. Stir and stir. Then test: dip another stick in. Pair it. Stir.

"Okay, Jim. Take half this green paint and git that wall there covered."

He hands me a clean brush, black bristles glistening with yesterday's thinner. He pours a gallon bucket full, deft tilt, and cuts the fall off clean.

"I'll be back in a minute," he says.

It's the first time I've painted anything away from home. I do not yet know that this wall is the beginning of the end, that before summer is out I will dread the look of yet another long, unpainted wall and wince at the smell of thinner. I want this one to be a good job. I want to live up to the paint he's just mixed. I start by the livingroom door, taking my time, keeping the molding clear for a white trim later.

Ten minutes pass, and this first wall becomes my world, each piece I cover is a quadrant on my map of it. I am moving across the wide-open middle country—working my brush like dad told me to the time we painted the back side of our house, using the wrist, lapping strokes over— when I feel compelled to turn around.

In the far doorway the lady of the house stands glaring at me, her eyes a blend of terror and hate. I realize how dangerous I must look to her: next to the wall of her priceless livingroom she finds Tom Sawyer with his cuffs rolled thick, whitewashing away an afternoon.

Under green freckles my face turns scarlet.

She disappears.

From the hallway comes her loud whisper. "Mr Houston! That boy painting my livingroom wall couldn't be over fifteen!"

"He's thirteen, Ma'am."

"He's what?"

"It's my boy, Jim. He's giving me a hand this summer."

"I just wonder if he knows what he's doing in there."

"I painted my first house when I was ten."

"Well . . . I . . . if . . . I'd certainly be keeping an eye on him if I were you."

"Don't worry, ma'am, he knows what to do."

Behind me I hear her walking slowly across the room. I keep painting, don't look at her this time. Plenty of paint on the brush. But don't let it run. Feather it at the overlap. Cover. Cover.

Dad comes in and fills up another gallon bucket and helps me finish the wall. He catches my eye once and winks at the fast one we have pulled on Mrs. So-and-so. Then we are covering the middle country together, in a curiously enclosed stillness, broken only by the whish of bristles and cluck of brush handle against the can. Somewhere in the back of the house a radio is playing, but its faraway music doesn't penetrate our territory.

We finish the room by quitting time. Dad looks over the sections I've painted, finds a couple of holidays along the baseboard and has me fill these in before we clean the brushes, saying only, "Keep an eye out for them holidays," and then a little later, when the sash tools are thinnered, and the pigment tubes lined up the way he wants them, next to the knives he uses for cutting linoleum and spreading putty and spackling cracks, he drops the lid shut on his kit of a suitcase, snaps the buckle to, straps it, says, "Might as well take that on out to the truck."

I have never paid much attention to his kit. Now I know just enough about what's inside for its contents to be mysteries. A year from now I will know too much about what's inside, and I will be able to read his half smile, already on the verge of apologizing for having only this to reward me with. But today it is an honor. No one has ever carried that kit but him. It has mysterious weight, with gypsy daubs of ivory, burnt umber and vermilion all across the ancient leather. A fine weight for carrying from the house downstairs to the curb.

At the county dump I am throwing away my father, hefting this suitcase to toss the last of him onto the smoking heap, when that shred of leather gives and the buckle breaks. The kit flies open. As if compressed inside, waiting to escape, the pungent smell of oil and rare pigments cuts through smoke and rot and fills the air around me. The few tubes still in there begin to topple. My throwing arm stays. My other hand reaches. I'm holding the suitcase, inhaling the smell that always surrounded him, even after he had scrubbed. It rose from the creases in his hands, from permanent white liners rimming his fingernails, from the paint-motes he sometimes missed with thinner, at the corners of his eyes.

I breathe deep. Close the suitcase slowly. Prepare to heave it once and for all. This time with both hands. Out among all those things you only find by losing them. Out and up. And onto the truck bed. Where it lands with a thunk. And sits solid. Those aromatic tubes give it density. I wait for him to tie his ladder on the overhead rack, and we climb into the cab. He winks once more, as we prepare to leave Mrs. So-and-so behind. Reeking of paint and turpentine, billcaps shoved back, we are Sherwin and Williams calling it a day, with no way to talk much over the stuttering engine of his metal-floored chevvy, and no need to talk. The sticky clutch leaps. Wind rushes in, mixing paint and gasoline fumes, and all you need to do is stay loose for the jolts and the whole long rumble ride home.

Santa Cruz, California
February 1987

Notes

Dreaming With Montalvo and Cortez

Montalvo's novel, LAS SERGAS DE ESPLANDIAN, was published in Spain in 1510. These excerpts come from Edward Everett Hale's 1872 translation, portions of which were reprinted as THE QUEEN OF CALIFORNIA, The Colt Press, San Francisco, 1945.

The Men In My Life

The story about George Hearst comes from W. A. Swanberg's biography, CITIZEN HEARST, Charles Scribners, New York, 1961.

The crows my grandmother sang about were originally "Three Ravens." The classic version, as recorded in F. J. Child's THE ENGLISH AND SCOTTISH POPULAR BALLADS, 1892-98, begins like this:

i

There were three ravens sat on a tree,
Down a down, hay down, hay down
There were three ravens sat on a tree,
With a down
There were three ravens sat on a tree,
They were as black as they might be.
With a down derry, derry, derry, down, down.

ii

The one of them said to his mate,
'Where shall we our breakfast take?' . . .

161

ABOUT THE AUTHOR

James D. Houston was born in San Francisco and has spent most of his life on the Pacific Coast, but he has deep roots in Texas, Tennessee and Alabama, as some of the stories in this collection reveal. He is the author of six novels, including the acclaimed *Continental Drift*, as well as several nonfiction works. He and his wife, Jeanne Wakatsuki Houston, co-authored *Farewell to Manzanar*, the story of a Japanese-American family during World War II, and adapted it for an NBC World Premier movie. Houston lives in Santa Cruz, where he occasionally offers writing workshops at the University of California and sits in from time to time with local country-western bands